SCIENCE DAYBOOK

In Collaboration with **NSTA**

D1534431

GReaT S#uRCe®
EDUCATION GROUP
A Division of Houghton Mifflin Company

Acknowledgments

Reviewers

Deb Barnes
6th Grade Science – Team 4
Fort Riley Middle School USD #475
Fort Riley, Kansas

Marilyn Cook
Teacher
Port Aransas ISD
Port Aransas, Texas

Charles Harmon
Science Teacher
Belvedere Middle School
Los Angeles Unified School District
Los Angeles, California

Marilyn R. LeRud
Retired Elementary Teacher
Tucson Unified School District
Tucson, Arizona

Maxine Rosenberg
Science Curriculum Consultant
Newton, Massachusetts

Dwight Sieggreen
Science Teacher
Hillside Middle School
Northville, Michigan

Nadine A. Solomon
Elementary Science Specialist
Arlington Public Schools
Arlington, Massachusetts

Richard Sturgeon
Teacher Earth/Space and Biology
Glastonbury High School
Glastonbury, Connecticut

Nancy Thornblad
Curriculum Facilitator
Millard Public Schools
Omaha, Nebraska

Thomas Vaughn
Lead Science Teacher
Arlington Public Schools
Arlington, Massachusetts

Karen Lang
Teacher
Monticello Central Schools
Monticello, New York

Credits

Writing: Sarah Martin, Marianne Knowles
Editorial: Molly F. Wetterschneider; Great Source: Claire Boivin, Kathy Kellman, Susan Rogalski
Design: Brown Publishing Network
Production Management: Great Source: Evelyn Curley
Cover Design: Brown Publishing Network

Cover
(c): ©Buddy Mays/CORBIS; (bml): © Ruth Cole/Animals, Animals/Earth Scenes; (bmr): ©Bill Lea/Dembinsky Photo Associates; (br): Fran Jarvis; (bl): ©Don Farrall/ PhotoDisc/Getty Images; (bkgrnd): ©Chris Collins/CORBIS

Photos
Page 20: ©M.J. O'Riain & J. Jarvis/Visuals Unlimited; 23: ©Wildlife Conservation Society, headquartered at the Bronx Zoo; 25: ©Adam Jones/Visuals Unlimited; 27: ©W. Perry Conway/CORBIS; 30(l): ©Joseph Van Os/Image Bank/Getty Images; 30(c): ©Ken Lucas/Taxi/Getty Images; 30(r): ©Carolina Biological/Visuals Unlimited; 32: Courtesy of Dr. Gavin Hunt; 41(t): ©Oliver J.Troisfontaines/SuperStock; 41(l): ©Barry Koffler/feathersite.com; 41(r): ©Barry Koffler/feathersite.com; 44: ©Sullivan and Rogers/Bruce Coleman, Inc.; 46: ©E.R. Derringer/Bruce Coleman, Inc.; 52: ©Arnold Genthe/Arnold Genthe Collection/Library of Congress; 53: ©Arnold Genthe/Arnold Genthe Collection/Library of Congress; 54: R. Decker/United States Geological Survey; 58: ©Hans Strand/Getty Images; 59: ©Ann and Peter Bosted; 64: ©Gerald French/ CORBIS; 65: ©Bettmann/CORBIS; 66: ©David Frazier/Photo Researchers, Inc.; 69: ©American Museum of Natural History/ neg. 5401; 76: ©DonFarrall/PhotoDisc/Getty Images; 77: ©Jim Reed/CORBIS; 82: ©Reynir Eyjolfsson; 84: ©Mike Brinson/ Image Bank/Getty Images; 85(l, c, r): ©Reynir Eyjolfsson; 90 (tr): ©Michael & Patricia Fogden/CORBIS; 90 (c): ©Buddy Mays/CORBIS; 90 (bl): ©David A. North-cott/CORBIS; 90(br): ©Kevin Schafer/CORBIS; 91: ©Michael & Patricia Fogden/CORBIS; 95: William L. Clements Library/The University of Michigan; 102: Bob Goldberg/ Feature Photo Service; 106: Courtesy of Pasco Scientific; 108: CORBIS; 109: Univer-sity of Kentucky Library; 114: Courtesy of Mohammed Bah Abba; 119: ©Nick Koudis/ Photodisc/Getty Images; 128: ©John Swedberg/Bruce Coleman, Inc.; 131 (l): ©Nigel Bean/naturepl.com (Nature Place); 131(r): ©Mark Edwards/Peter Arnold, Inc.; 133: Courtesy of Dr. Joseph Kiesecker/Penn State University; 134: ©Sheldon Allen Blake/Animals Animals, Earth Scenes; 135: ©Annette Coolridge/Photo Edit, Inc.; 136: ©Randy M. Ury/CORBIS; 137: ©Bill Lea/Dembinsky Photo Associates; 143: ©Hulton–Deutsch/ CORBIS; 144: ©Sheila Terry/Photo Researchers, Inc.; 147: ©Royalty-free/CORBIS; 150: ©Richard Shell/Animals Animals/Earth Scenes; 155: Photo courtesy of Sylvia Campbell/NIWRA; 158: Photo courtesy of Sylvia Campbell/ NIWRA; 159: THE INCREDIBLE HULK: TM & ©2005 Marvel Characters, Inc. Used with permission; 160: Courtesy of Universal Studios Licensing LLLP

Illustration
Pages 6, 21: Gene Barretta; 13, 35, 43, 48, 51, 63, 81, 113, 139: Amy Vangsgard; 14, 15: Lane Smith; 17, 18, 37: Grace Lin; 19, 103: Jessica Flick; 22: Barroux; 26, 27, 34: Tammy Smith; 28: Linda Bleck; 29, 61, 83 (all), 93, 97 (t), 99, 100, 111, 123, 151, 152: Mike Wesley; 31, 75, 89, 101, 107, 119, 127: ©Linda Bronson; 38, 39: Louis Darling; 55, 56, 129 (t): Sophie Kitteridge; 67 (all): Fran Jarvis; 71, 73 (t), 114, 115, 116, 153: Viviana Garofoli; 73 (b): Teen Liu; 79 (l, r): Doug Ross; 97 (b): © Dean Stanton; 105, 112, 121 (br, cr), 124: Roberto Sabas; 120, 142: Shennen Bersani; 122: Armstrong Sperry; 129 (b), 161: Pamela Thomson; 132 (l, r): Ann Barrow; 138, 140: Kristen Balouch; 149: John O'Brien; 164: Jason Peltz.

National Science Teachers Association:
Dave Anderson, Tyson Brown, Carol Duval, Carole Hayward, Caryn Long, Pat Warren

SciLINKS® is a registered trademark of the National Science Teachers Association. The SciLINKS® service includes copyrighted materials and is owned and provided by the National Science Teachers Association. All Rights Reserved.

Copyright © 2004 by Great Source Education Group, a division of Houghton Mifflin Company. All rights reserved.

No part of this work may be reproduced or transmitted in any form or by any means, electronic or mechanical, including photocopying and recording, or by any information storage or retrieval system, without the prior written permission of Great Source Education Group, unless such copying is expressly permitted by federal copyright law. Address inquiries to Permissions, Great Source Education Group, 181 Ballardvale Street, Wilmington, MA 01887.

Great Source ® and ScienceSaurus ® are registered trademarks of Houghton Mifflin Company.

All registered trademarks are shown strictly for illustrative purposes and are the property of their respective owners.

Printed in the United States of America
International Standard Book Number: 0-669-51165-X
1 2 3 4 5 6 7 8 9 10 QWV 08 07 06 05 04

Contents

UNIT 1: Life Science

UNIT 2: Earth Science

UNIT 3: Physical Science

UNIT 4: Natural Resources and the Environment

UNIT 5: Science, Technology and Society

What Is a Science Daybook?

A *Science Daybook* is a workbook that brings together science, reading, and writing. This *Science Daybook* is your very own and, as you use it, you may mark it up with pens and pencils and markers. The more you make it your own, the more valuable the *Daybook* will be to you.

About the Daybook Readings

Each chapter in this book is based on one or two readings. The readings come from a wide variety of sources, including science books, magazines, newspapers, radio shows, web sites, literature, and poetry. Yes, poetry! That's because science is everywhere, not just in science books. (The sources in this book are listed on pages 173 and 174.)

What's in a Daybook Chapter?

Each *Science Daybook* chapter is six pages long. Every chapter begins with the same parts: an introduction, Before You Read, and Read. What comes after Read depends on the chapter. Before You Read is described below. The following pages describe all the other kinds of sections you'll find in a chapter.

Before You Read

Each chapter begins with a quick Before You Read feature. As you might expect, this feature gets you to think about the topic of the reading, before you start reading it.

Read

Every chapter in the *Science Daybook* is built around one or two readings. You are encouraged to read the *Daybook* actively. What does it mean to be an active reader? It means that as you read, you are actively marking up the text—writing notes, drawing diagrams, jotting down questions. The more involved you are with the readings in this book, the better you will understand them.

notes:

Jot down your ideas, questions, and drawings in the Notes columns. At the bottom of each column are a few directions or questions. These help you to find the science in the reading.

Vocabulary

Words underlined in the reading are defined at the bottom of the page.

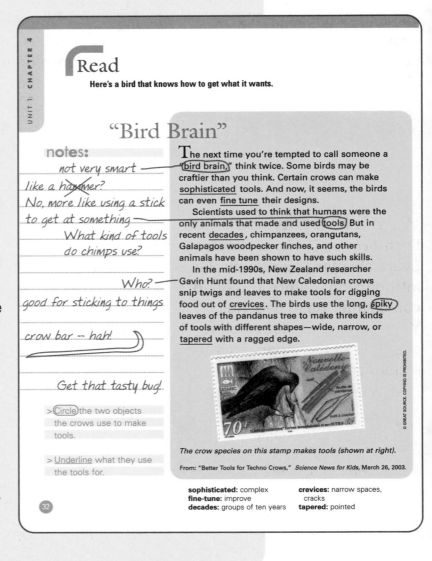

After the Read section, you will find other kinds of features and activities. These features help you to understand the science related to the reading.

Look Back

> Most chapters have a Look Back feature following each reading. Look Back questions help you to notice something important from the reading.

Explore

In Explore, you might answer questions, interpret a diagram, analyze data, or explore a science topic from the reading in some other way.

Glossary Look up unfamiliar words in the glossary on pages 166–172. The glossary gives a simple definition for each word and gives you a chapter page where you can learn more about it.

---

erosion: the movement of weathered rock by water, wind, or ice **(62, 66)**

Activity

Some chapters invite you to do a hands-on activity. Always read the whole activity and get all your materials before you begin. Be sure to follow any special directions from your teacher, along with the ones on the page.

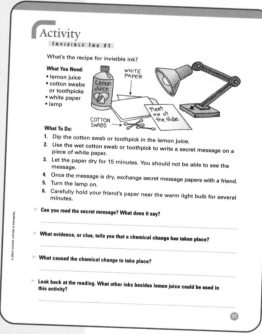

Science Journal

In this feature, you may be asked to keep a record of science observations, write an essay about topics discussed in the chapter, or write a letter about your experiences with a science topic.

Project

In a Project, you might be asked to research a science topic further, make a display, or make observations of your local area, and report on what you find out.

Put It All Together

Chapters that have two readings often end with this feature. The two readings are related, and Put It All Together helps you make the connection between them.

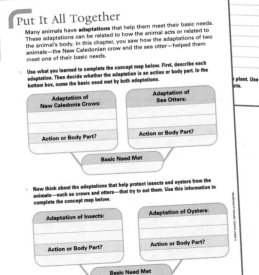

More Resources

ScienceSaurus is a reference book written for students like you. It's filled with information about all kinds of science subjects. It also has instructions about doing science activities, writing up science reports, doing library and internet research, and preparing for tests. Whether you want to know about animals, rocks, machines, weather, or many other subjects, turn to *ScienceSaurus*.

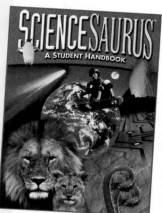

Every chapter in the *Science Daybook* has references to pages in *ScienceSaurus*. The references appear on the first page of the chapter, next to Before You Read. Look on these pages in *ScienceSaurus* for information related to the *Daybook* chapter.

www.scilinks.org	web address for *Sci*LINKS
Keyword: Behavior	science subject for this link
Code: GSLD12	code to type in at the *Sci*LINKS web site

What is a *Sci*LINK? A *Sci*LINK is a "science link" between a subject you are studying and web sites where you can learn more about the subject.

Most chapters in this *Science Daybook* have at least one *Sci*LINK. The *Sci*LINKS appear on the first page of the chapter, next to Before You Read.

How to use *Sci*LINKS
1. Go to the *Sci*LINKS web site at www.SciLINKS.org.
2. After you register, sign in by entering your user name and password.
3. Type in the code for the keyword you want to know more about.
4. You will see a list of different web sites that discuss that keyword subject. Click on one of the addresses to get to the site.
5. Go back to the *Sci*LINKS web site and try a different web site.

UNIT 1: Life Science

DID YOU KNOW?
Some plants are able to capture and digest insects. One of these plants is called the Venus Fly Trap.

Chapter 1 Ladybugs Galore
Find Out: How do scientists tell one kind of ladybug from another?

Chapter 2 Mole-rat-unculus
Find Out: Which parts of a mole-rat's body are most sensitive to touch?

Chapter 3 Fierce Plants
Find Out: Why do some plants eat insects?

Chapter 4 Nature's Toolbox
Find Out: Which animals use tools to help them get food?

Chapter 5
Are You My Mother?
Find Out: Can a chicken lay an egg that doesn't contain a chick?

Chapter 6 Out of Control
Find Out: What if the solution to one environmental problem creates another?

Are all ladybugs alike?

Here's a challenge: how long would it take you to name every kind of living thing on Earth? Do you think it would take all day? Actually, it could take you months! That's because there are millions of kinds of living things on Earth.

It could take you quite a while just to name the kinds of ladybugs. Ladybugs are a type of insect. You may think all ladybugs are alike, but did you know that there are 450 different kinds of ladybugs in North America? In fact, there are 4500 kinds of ladybugs worldwide. That's a lot of ladybugs!

In this chapter, you'll learn how scientists tell one kind of ladybug from another.

Before You Read

You've probably seen a ladybug walking up the stalk of a garden plant or trapped inside a screen door. Close your eyes and try to remember what it looked like. Draw the ladybug in the space below.

SCIENCESAURUS
A STUDENT HANDBOOK
BLUE BOOK

Species .... p. 128
Animals ...... p. 141
Animals With an
Exoskeleton p. 148

SCi LINKS.
THE WORLD'S A CLICK AWAY

www.scilinks.org
Keyword:
Classification
Code: GS5D005

Read

Seven-year-old James Henry Trotter is on a fantastical journey with a group of animal friends—a grasshopper, a spider, a centipede, a glow-worm, an earthworm, and a ladybug. Sailing through the skies aboard the Giant Peach, James has a chance to ask the ladybug about her spots.

"A Fine Thing To Be"

notes:

> Do all ladybugs have the same number of spots?

> Underline what a ladybug's spots tell you about her.

"I think you're wonderful," James told her. "Can I ask you one special question?"

"Please do."

"Well, is it really true that I can tell how old a Ladybug is by counting her spots?"

"Oh no, that's just a children's story," the Ladybug said. "We never change our spots. Some of us, of course, are born with more spots than others, but we never change them. The number of spots that a Ladybug has is simply a way of showing which branch of the family she belongs to. I, for example, as you can see for yourself, am a Nine-Spotted Ladybug. I am very lucky. It is a fine thing to be."

"It is, indeed," said James, gazing at the beautiful <u>scarlet</u> shell with the nine black spots on it.

"On the other hand," the Ladybug went on, "some of my less fortunate relatives have no more than two spots altogether on their shells! Can you imagine that? They are called Two-Spotted Ladybugs, and very common and ill-mannered they are, I regret to say. And then, of course, you have the Five-Spotted Ladybugs as well. They are much nicer than the Two-Spotted ones, although I myself find them a <u>trifle</u> too <u>saucy</u> for my taste."

"But they are all of them loved?" said James.

"Yes," the Ladybug answered quietly. "They are all of them loved."

From: *James and the Giant Peach* by Roald Dahl.

notes:

> List three kinds of ladybugs described in the reading.

scarlet: red
trifle: little
saucy: disrespectful

Look Back

A **trait** is a characteristic or feature, such as having brown hair or having two eyes.

> **What trait was used to tell one kind of ladybug from the other?**

Explore

CLASSIFY LADYBUGS

Scientists divide living things into groups based on their traits. These groups form a **classification system.** A classification system makes it easier to see how all living things are related to one another. For example, mammals, insects, and birds all belong to a group that includes all animals. Scientists divide the insect group into even smaller groups. Look at the diagram below. It shows some of the different groups of living things within the animal group.

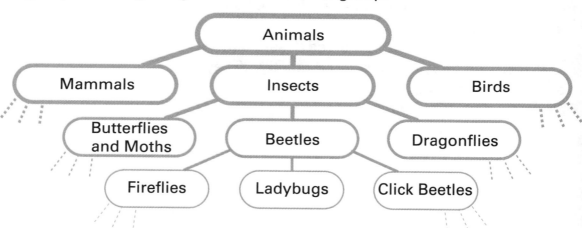

> **Color in all the groups that the ladybugs belong to.**

> **What is the largest group that the ladybugs belong to?**

> **Now add to the diagram ovals for the three kinds of ladybugs described in the reading. Which group should they branch off from? Label your new ovals.**

Explore

The smallest group that a living thing can belong to is called a species. A **species** is one kind of living thing. For example, the gray wolf is one kind of species. The two-spotted ladybug is another. Only two living things of the same species can mate with each other and produce more members of that species. Look at the pictures of three species of ladybugs, below. How are the ladybugs alike? How are they different?

Two-Spotted Ladybug *Five-Spotted Ladybug* *Nine-Spotted Ladybug*

> **Complete the Venn diagram below to show which traits are unique to each species of ladybug and which traits are shared by all three species.**

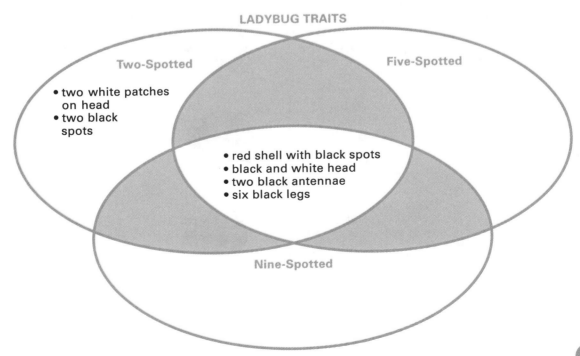

LADYBUG TRAITS

Two-Spotted
- two white patches on head
- two black spots

Five-Spotted

- red shell with black spots
- black and white head
- two black antennae
- six black legs

Nine-Spotted

Explore

WHAT'S IN A NAME?

Each species has a special scientific name. These names may look strange or unfamiliar to you because they use words from languages that people used long ago—such as Latin and Ancient Greek.

For example, the name that scientists use for the ladybug family is "Coccinellidae." Look at the first part of the name: "Cocc-." Replace the "c"s with "k"s. You get "Kokk-." The Greek word *kokkos* means "berry." So the family name for ladybug comes from the Greek word for "berry."

> **Why do you think they used the word "berry" to name the ladybug family?**

_____

_____

_____

Knowing some Latin and Greek word parts can help you understand scientific names. Look at the chart below of Latin word parts for numbers.

> **Use the information in the chart to match each ladybug to its correct scientific name. (Hint: How many spots does each ladybug have?)**

Number	Word Part
1	un-
2	du-, di-, bi
3	tre-
4	quat-
5	quin-
6	sex-
7	sept-
8	oct-
9	nov-
10	dec-

Coccinella **nov**emnotata

Adalia **bi**punctata

Hippodamia **quin**quesignata

If you were a naked mole-rat, how would you find your way around the pitch-black tunnels of your home?

Do you know what a naked mole-rat looks like? Well, you can probably guess that it doesn't have a lot of hair! The naked mole-rat is a small, nearly hairless mammal that lives underground in tunnels. Its whole life is spent in the dark. Unfortunately, it hasn't learned how to use a flashlight, so it has to move around and do all the things it does in total darkness.

In this chapter, you'll read about some scientists who studied the naked mole-rat. They wanted to find out how the naked mole-rat is able to get around so well in the pitch dark.

Before You Read

Smell is one of the senses—touch, taste, smell, sight, and hearing. Imagine that you are standing alone in a house you've never been in before.

> **What senses would you use to get information about your surroundings? What sense would you probably not use?**

_____

_____

_____

> **Now imagine that all the lights have been turned off and your ears have been plugged. Which senses would be most useful now?**

_____

_____

Sensing the Environment p. 90
Sense Organs .... p. 125

www.scilinks.org
Keyword:
Adaptations of Animals
Code: GS5D010

Read

Meet the naked mole-rat. It may not be pretty, but it's pretty cool. Find out why this animal is more likely to touch teeth with another naked mole-rat than shake hands.

"Night of the Living Unculus"

notes:

> Which of the senses would be most important to an animal living in a place with no light and little sound?

> How does the size of the body part in the "touch map" relate to the number of nerve cells in the actual body part?

You've probably never asked yourself what it feels like to be a naked mole-rat. Scientists have found out anyway. And they're just bursting to tell you, so here goes.

The naked mole-rat is a <u>bizarre</u> East African beast that spends most of its life <u>scurrying</u> through burrows underground. In order to be a champion tunnel runner, it is nearly hairless and has small eyes and ears. It has been called a hot-dog with teeth, but frankly, we think that's being kind. It's way too ugly to be food.

This past April scientists reported that they had mapped the part of the mole-rat's brain that responds to touch. They put tiny <u>electrodes</u> into the mole-rat's brain, touched a part of its body, and recorded which nerve cells fired. After they had completed the experiment, they drew a naked mole-rat ["touch map"]. The more nerve cells

bizarre: weird
scurrying: running

electrodes: tiny devices that are used to record electrical signals

The Moleratunculus

[the body part had], the bigger they drew the part. The scientific name for this kind of touch map in people is *homunculus*, which is Latin for "little man." So the scientists called their map a moleratunculus. Guess which part of the mole-ratunculus is the biggest?

Fully a third of the mole-rat's "<u>touch cortex</u>" is devoted to those fantastic front choppers, which it uses for eating, digging, dragging things around, and socializing with other mole-rats. In fact, the teeth seem to have taken over an area of the brain devoted to vision in [animals] that are similar but do not spend their lives in the dark.

From: "Night of the Living Unculus," *Muse* magazine, February 2003.

touch cortex: part of the brain that receives information about touch

> <u>Underline</u> what the naked mole-rat uses its teeth for.

Look Back

Look at the following two terms from the reading.

Homunculus   Moleratunculus

> Underline the group of letters that both terms have in common.

> What does a "touch map"—or unculus—show?

_____

_____

_____

_____

_____

> What does a homunculus show?

_____

_____

_____

_____

> What does a moleratunculus show?

_____

_____

_____

_____

Explore

Look at the photo of the naked mole-rat at right. Now look back at the mole-ratunculus shown on page 21.

Look at the naked mole-rat's body parts in the photo. Now compare the size of these parts to the same parts in the moleratunculus.

> **What do you notice?**

_____

_____

> **According to the moleratunculus, which parts of the naked mole-rat are most sensitive and have the most nerve cells?**

_____

_____

> **Why do you think these parts of the naked mole-rat are the most sensitive to touch? (Hint: Think about how the naked mole-rat moves around in its environment.)**

_____

_____

_____

_____

_____

Explore

DRAWING A HOMUNCULUS

In the human body, the lips, tongue, hands, fingers, and thumbs are the most sensitive to touch.

> **Why do you think these parts of a human are most sensitive to touch?**

_____

_____

_____

_____

_____

_____

> **Use what you have learned about "touch maps" to draw a homunculus. Which parts of the human body are bigger on the homunculus?**

Fierce Plants

Chapter 3

Some plants have to get tough to meet their needs.

Like all living things, plants have basic needs that have to be met in order for them to survive. You probably know that plants need water, but water is just one of a plant's basic needs. You will learn about some other needs in this chapter. For example, a plant also needs energy, minerals, and protection from animals that want to eat it.

The environment where a plant grows must supply the plant with all of its needs or the plant will die. Some environments are better than others. Think about a weed growing in a small crack in the sidewalk. The soil is not very deep or rich, and the sidewalk is hot. The weed must be able to deal with the harsh environment where it lives. In places where the environment is not ideal, plants have special ways to meet their needs. In this chapter, you will learn about these types of plants.

Before You Read

A cactus is a kind of plant. Cactuses grow mainly in deserts. The desert environment is very dry because it does not rain very often or very much. Plants that grow in deserts have to store as much water as they can between rainfalls. Desert animals will often eat these plants in order to get at the stored water. A cactus needs to protect itself from animals.

> **Look at the picture of the cactus. What structures protect the cactus from animals?**

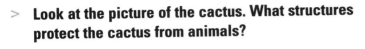

SCIENCESAURUS
A STUDENT HANDBOOK
BLUE BOOK

Organism's Basic Needs .... p. 76
Adaptations p. 77
Getting and Using Energy .... p. 77
Photosynthesis .... p. 80

SCLINKS.
THE WORLD'S A CLICK AWAY

www.scilinks.org
Keyword: Adaptations of Plants
Code: GS5D015

Read

Hosts Don Glass and Yael Ksander discuss the Venus Fly Trap on their radio show, *A Moment of Science*.

"What the Heck Is It?"

notes:

> How is a Venus Fly Trap classified?

> How is a plant defined?

Don: Today, on a Moment of Science, it's time for another round of "What the Heck Is It?", that fun and wacky <u>classification</u> game. Please welcome—all the way from Bloomington, Indiana—today's contestant, Yael Ksander.
  [APPLAUSE]

Yael: Thanks, Don. Glad to be here.

Don: Are you ready, Yael?

Yael: Sure am.

Don: Okay, Listen carefully. What the heck is a— Venus Fly Trap?

Yael: Hmm! Is it a type of plant?
  [APPLAUSE]

Don: That's right! You get to move on to the next question! Ready?

Yael: Yes.

Don: Okay! What the heck is a plant?

Yael: Plants are defined as organisms that use photosynthesis to produce their own food. Photosynthesis is the process by which plants use light to convert water and carbon dioxide into simple sugars.

Don: That's 2 out of 3!
  [APPLAUSE] And now, the grand prize question [OOO!]
Everyone knows that the Venus Fly Trap catches and <u>consumes</u> small insects. So, how the heck can the Venus Fly Trap be a plant if it's a <u>carnivore</u>?

classification: system of organizing living things into different groups

consumes: eats
carnivore: an organism that eats animals

Yael: Simple, Don. Carnivorous plants still rely on photosynthesis as their main source of energy. However, because they grow in areas where the soil <u>lacks</u> <u>essential</u> nutrients, they use the insects they capture as a source of nitrogen and other minerals. So the Venus Fly Trap doesn't technically eat the insects—that is, it doesn't <u>convert</u> the insects into energy—and it definitely couldn't survive on insects alone. [APPLAUSE]

Don: You did it, Yael! You've won our grand prize! Congratulations! Please join us next time for another round of "What the Heck Is It?"

From: "What the Heck Is a Venus Fly Trap?"
A Moment of Science, Radio Station WFIU and Indiana University.

notes:

lacks: doesn't have
essential: important
convert: change

Look Back

Like all plants, the Venus Fly Trap uses photosynthesis to get the energy that it needs. Plants also need essential nutrients, such as minerals and nitrogen. Usually plants get these nutrients from soil.

> **How does the Venus Fly Trap get minerals and nitrogen?**

Explore

PLANT OR ANIMAL?

According to the reading, the Venus Fly Trap does some "animal-like" things.

> **Name an "animal-like" thing that the Venus Fly Trap does.**

But scientists still classify the Venus Fly Trap as a plant, not an animal.

> **Why do scientists classify the Venus Fly Trap as a plant if it does "animal-like" things? What makes it a plant?**

"My homework ate my dog!"

EATING INSECTS

You might wonder how the Venus Fly Trap "eats" an insect. It doesn't chew the insect up and swallow it as an animal would. The three steps described below show how a Venus Fly Trap gets nutrients from insects:

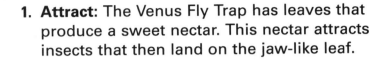

1. **Attract:** The Venus Fly Trap has leaves that produce a sweet nectar. This nectar attracts insects that then land on the jaw-like leaf.

2. **Trap:** When an insect steps on the "trigger hairs" inside the leaf, the two halves of the leaf instantly close over the insect. Long spines on the edges of the leaf trap the insect inside.

3. **Digest and Absorb:** Glands in the leaf give off juices that digest the soft parts of the insect, leaving the hard parts. The nutrients from the insect's body are soaked up by the leaf trap.

> **Fill in the chart below to show the function of each step and the plant structure that is used to carry out that function. The first box has been done for you.**

Step	Function	Plant Structure that Serves this Function
1	Attract insect	
2		
3		

Project

CARNIVOROUS BOG PLANTS

Have you ever seen a Venus Fly Trap growing in the wild? You probably haven't. That's because they grow only in bogs found in a few small areas of North Carolina and South Carolina. A bog is an area of land where the soil is very wet and swampy and usually lacks the nitrogen and minerals that plants need to live. The Venus Fly Trap has adapted to life in the bog by being a carnivorous plant. But the Venus Fly Trap is not the only bog plant that "eats" insects.

> **Research another carnivorous plant that grows in bogs. Here are some choices:**

1. Pitcher plant   **2.** Sundew   **3.** Bladderwort

   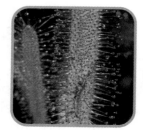   

> **How does the plant attract, trap, digest, and absorb insects? What structures does it have to carry out these functions? Record what you find in your research.**

_____

_____

_____

_____

_____

_____

_____

_____

_____

> **Now make a poster showing what you found out about your carnivorous plant. Use pictures and words to describe how the plant captures and digests insects.**

How can you get at a tasty bug hiding in a narrow crack?

Imagine that you are getting dressed in a hurry one morning. As you grab for your socks, one accidentally slips across your dresser and falls behind it. Uh-oh. The dresser is far too heavy to move. How can you get your sock?

Believe it or not, birds often find themselves facing that same question. Well, they don't wear socks, but they do hunt for insects. These insects are often hiding in hard-to-reach places to protect themselves.

In this lesson, you'll read about a type of bird that found an original way to pick a meal out of a tight space. You'll also learn how sea otters get a meal out of another kind of "tight space."

Before You Read

Can you think of a time when you got something out of a tight space or somewhere that was hard to reach? How did you do it? Did you use another object to help you?

SCIENCE SAURUS
A STUDENT HANDBOOK
BLUE BOOK

Adaptations p. 77
Animal
Behavior ...... p. 93

SC LINKS.
THE WORLD'S A CLICK AWAY

www.scilinks.org
Keyword:
Behaviors, and
Adaptations
Code: GS5D020

> **Describe your experience with sentences or drawings.**

⌐Read

Here's a bird that knows how to get what it wants.

"Bird Brain"

notes:

The next time you're tempted to call someone a "bird brain," think twice. Some birds may be craftier than you think. Certain crows can make <u>sophisticated</u> tools. And now, it seems, the birds can even <u>fine tune</u> their designs.

Scientists used to think that humans were the only animals that made and used tools. But in recent <u>decades</u>, chimpanzees, orangutans, Galapagos woodpecker finches, and other animals have been shown to have such skills.

In the mid-1990s, New Zealand researcher Gavin Hunt found that New Caledonian crows snip twigs and leaves to make tools for digging food out of <u>crevices</u>. The birds use the long, spiky leaves of the pandanus tree to make three kinds of tools with different shapes—wide, narrow, or <u>tapered</u> with a ragged edge.

> Circle the two objects the crows use to make tools.

> Underline what they use the tools for.

The crow species on this stamp makes tools (shown at right).

From: "Better Tools for Techno Crows," *Science News for Kids*, March 26, 20

sophisticated: complex
fine-tune: improve
decades: groups of ten years

crevices: narrow spaces, cracks
tapered: pointed

Look Back

> **What problem did the New Caledonian crows face? What solution did they find? What tool was part of their solution?**

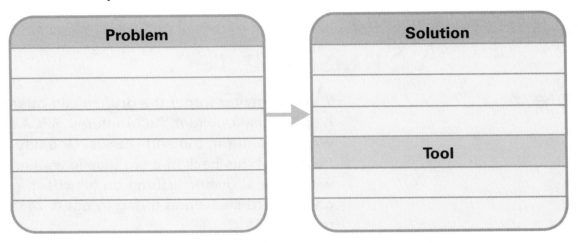

Problem

Solution

Tool

Explore

WHY USE A TOOL?

Like all animals, crows have basic needs that they have to meet in order to survive. These needs include food, water, air, and shelter.

> **How did the crows use the pandanus leaves to help them get food?**

_____

_____

_____

> **Look at the leaf tools shown in the picture on the previous page. Why might these leaves make good tools for digging in crevices?**

_____

> **A tool is a device that is used to make a job easier. How do the leaves that the crows cut fit the definition of a tool?**

_____

_____

Read

Crows aren't the only animals that use tools. Newspaper writer Gary Bogue remembers the time he saw a young sea otter wrestle with a difficult meal.

"A Smashing Idea"

notes:

> Circle the first thing the otter did to try to get inside the oyster.

> Why do you think the otter put the stone in its armpit?

And I'll never forget the orphan sea otter pup I helped raise down at the Monterey SPCA's wildlife center in the early 1980s. One day he was floating on his back in a big plastic wading pool with several oysters sitting on his chest, gnawing on the hard shells and trying to get to the tasty meat inside.

I heard a sudden banging sound and turned to see the otter pounding on one of the oysters with a smooth rock. That was curious because there hadn't been a rock in the pool. I turned my head for a moment and when I looked back, the rock was gone and the otter was eating the oyster.

I checked the pool out thoroughly and no rock. Following up on a hunch, I started to frisk the otter ("Stop, that tickles!"). I found the smooth stone tucked carefully in the otter's right front armpit. He let out a loud chatter until I gave it back.

The sea otter was using the rock as a tool to crack open the shells of the oysters and other shellfish we were feeding him.

From: *Pets and Wildlife* column, Contra Costa Times, April 16, 2003.

SPCA: Society for the Prevention of Cruelty to Animals
oysters: a type of shellfish
gnawing: biting and chewing

Look Back

> What problem did the sea otter face? What solution did it find? What tool was part of its solution?

Problem

Solution

Tool

Explore

M E E T I N G   N E E D S

Look at the picture of the sea otter floating in the ocean. Sea otters are able to float on their backs very comfortably for a long time.

> How does the otter use floating on its back to help it get food?

Put It All Together

Many animals have **adaptations** that help them meet their basic needs. These adaptations can be related to how the animal acts or related to the animal's body. In this chapter, you saw how the adaptations of two animals—the New Caledonian crow and the sea otter—helped them meet one of their basic needs.

> **Use what you learned to complete the concept map below. First, describe each adaptation. Then decide whether the adaptation is an action or body part. In the bottom box, name the basic need met by both adaptations.**

Adaptation of New Caledonia Crows:	Adaptation of Sea Otters:
Action or Body Part?	**Action or Body Part?**

Basic Need Met

> **Now think about the adaptations that help protect insects and oysters from the animals—such as crows and otters—that try to eat them. Use this information to complete the concept map below.**

Adaptation of Insects:	Adaptation of Oysters:
Action or Body Part?	**Action or Body Part?**

Basic Need Met

Can you hatch a dinosaur?

Do you know where babies come from? Well, from their parents, of course! All living things come from other living things—their parents. That's why **offspring**, or young, look like their parents.

Adult animals mate and reproduce to make more of their own kind. An animal can mate and reproduce only with another member of its same species, or kind. So, cats cannot mate with dogs and produce some sort of crazy cat-dog animal. They can mate only with other cats and produce baby cats.

In this chapter, you'll read a story about a mother hen and her most unusual offspring.

Before You Read

> **Look at the pictures below. Draw lines matching the offspring with their parents.**

SCIENCESAURUS — A STUDENT HANDBOOK — **BLUE BOOK**

Reproduction p. 82

> **What did you base your matches on?**

www.scilinks.org
Keyword: Traits
Code: GS5D030

Read

For weeks, Nate Twitchell has been helping a tired mother hen take care of her enormous egg. Early one morning, Nate goes to check on the egg in its nest.

"It Can't Be True..."

notes:

I just went over to the nest and put a little grain down for that poor old hen, and started to turn away, when I realized all at once that something had changed. The hen wasn't sitting on the nest anymore. She was walking back and forth with a kind of wild look in her eye, and every time she came near the nest she gave a little hop and fluttered away again. I bent down to look in the nest, and—wow! There was something in there, and it was alive! It was moving around.

I thought at first that it was a rat or something that had busted the egg and eaten it. But after I got a good look I could see that it wasn't any rat. It was about the size of a squirrel, but it didn't have any hair, and its head—well, I couldn't believe my eyes when I saw it. It didn't look like anything I'd ever seen before. It had three little knobs sticking out of its head and a sort of collar up over its neck. It was a lizardy-looking critter, and it kept moving its thick tail slowly back and forth in the nest. The poor hen was looking pretty upset. I guess she hadn't expected anything like this, and neither had I.

> What did the animal in the nest look like? <u>Underline</u> the words that describe its appearance.

Nate telephones rare egg expert Dr. Ziemer, who has asked Nate to call him the minute the egg hatches out.

Dr. Ziemer. . . ran up to the nest and looked in. His eyes opened up wide and he knelt down on the ground and stared and stared and stared. After a long while he said softly, "That's it. By George, that's just what it is." Then he stared for another long time and finally he shook his head and said, "It can't be true, but there it is."

He got up off his knees and looked around at us. His eyes were just sparkling, he was so excited. He put his hand on my shoulder, and I could feel he was <u>quivering</u>. "An amazing thing's happened," he said, in a kind of whisper. "I don't know how to <u>account for</u> it. It must be some sort of freak <u>biological</u> mixup that might happen once in a thousand years."

"But what is it?" I asked.

Dr. Ziemer turned and pointed a trembling finger at the nest. "Believe it or not, you people have hatched out a *dinosaur*."

From: *The Enormous Egg* by Oliver Butterworth.

notes:

> Why do you think Dr. Ziemer said "It can't be true..."?

> What explanation did Dr. Ziemer give for what he saw? <u>Underline</u> the answer.

quivering: shaking
account for: explain
biological: having to do with living things

Look Back

Nature is full of surprises. But it follows some basic rules. One rule is that all adult animals (parents) reproduce to make more young (offspring) of their own kind.

> **How do you know that the story you just read isn't really true?**

_____

_____

Explore

INHERITING TRAITS

Offspring **inherit,** or receive, traits from their parents. You inherited lots of basic traits from both of your parents. For example, you were born with two arms and two legs and two eyes, just like your parents. You don't have feathers or a tail. Neither do your parents.

> **Think about the traits of a chicken. List at least six traits of a chicken below.**

_____

_____

_____

> **Now list six traits of a dinosaur, like the one shown in reading.**

_____

_____

_____

> **Which traits are unique to a dinosaur? Could it inherit those traits from a chicken?**

_____

_____

_____

_____

Explore

Offspring look basically like their parents. But that doesn't mean that every offspring looks *exactly* like its parents. Variety among offspring is perfectly normal. For example, the photograph at right shows a mother hen with her six chicks. Notice that they don't all look exactly alike.

Mother hen with chicks

Because offspring inherit traits from both of their parents, they don't look exactly like either parent. Sometimes a mutation can make offspring look even more different. A **mutation** is a change in traits that happens when the traits are being passed from parent to offspring.

Look at the two pictures at right. The first shows a normal chicken. The second shows the same kind of chicken with a mutation known as "frizzles." This mutation causes the chicken's feathers to curve outward.

Normal   *Frizzles*

> **How is the "frizzles" chicken different from the "normal" chicken? How are they alike?**

_____

_____

_____

> **Mutations usually change one trait in an offspring, not many traits. Could a dinosaur be a mutant chicken?**

_____

_____

_____

Science Journal

> Imagine that you have been asked by the author of *The Enormous Egg* to write another version of the story. In the new version, Dr. Ziemer explains to Nate why a dinosaur could not hatch from a chicken egg. Write your explanation in the voice of Dr. Ziemer. Pick up the dialogue after Dr. Ziemer's remark "It can't be true..."

Then he stared for another long time and finally he shook his head and said, "It can't be true . . .

What's big and green and can take over the whole neighborhood?

If you've ever flipped through an encyclopedia, you know that Earth is home to millions of different species, or kinds, of living things. But not every kind of living thing is found in every place. Each area of the world has its own set of living things. Those living things are part of the area's unique ecosystem. An **ecosystem** is all of the living and non-living things that are found in an area.

For hundreds of years, people have taken plants and animals from one area and brought them to another. Species of plants and animals that have lived in an area for a very long time are called **native** species. Species that have been brought to a new area are called **introduced**, or non-native species. In this chapter, you will learn about what happened when two introduced species—one plant and one animal—were brought to ecosystems where they didn't normally live.

Before You Read

Imagine that you have a large aquarium with several pet goldfish. One day, your friend gives you an angelfish. You put the angelfish in the aquarium, but the next day you realize that the angelfish ate all of your goldfish!

> **In this story, which species of fish is the *native* species?**

_____

_____

> **Which species of fish is the *introduced* species?**

_____

_____

SCIENCESAURUS
A STUDENT HANDBOOK
BLUE BOOK

SCI LINKS.
THE WORLD'S A CLICK AWAY

www.scilinks.org
Keyword: Changes
in Ecosystems
Code: GS5D035

Read

Read about a Japanese vine that ended up doing more harm than good.

"Kudzu All Over You"

notes:

Often humans don't understand that a change they make in the environment may have a very different result from what they expected. The web of nature is complicated!

In the 1930s the government wanted to control soil erosion in the southern United States. So it hired hundreds of workers to plant fields of kudzu, a beautiful vine that is native to Japan. Big mistake! Without Japan's cooler climate and kudzu-munching beetles to keep the plant <u>in check</u>, kudzu grew out of control. Today it's an expensive problem. Kudzu covers millions of acres of land, <u>smothering</u> native trees and plants.

From: "Big Mistakes!," *ASK* magazine, July/Aug 2003

> <u>Underline</u> the two factors that keep kudzu under control in Japan.

in check: under control
smothering: growing over and killing

Look Back

What was the original problem faced by people in the United States? What solution did they find? What new problem did this solution create?

> **Complete the graphic organizer based on information from the reading.**

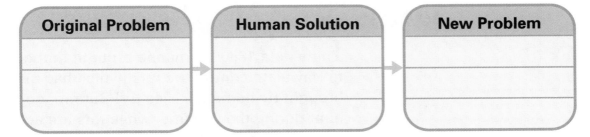

Original Problem	Human Solution	New Problem

Explore

STAYING BALANCED

All living things in an ecosystem interact with one another in a balanced way. That means that one group of living things does not grow out of control and destroy other groups of living things. This balance exists because they have lived together for many generations.

> **Why didn't the kudzu grow out of control in Japan? Describe the balance that existed between kudzu and the ecosystem where it grew.**

> **Why was the kudzu able to grow out of control in the new ecosystem?**

> **Why would it not be a good idea to bring in kudzu-eating beetles to control the kudzu?**

Read

It is not just introduced plants that can cause problems for native species. Read about an animal whose eating habits created serious problems for a native bird.

"Mongoose on the Loose"

notes:

In the late 1880s someone brought mongooses to Hawaii to control the rats (which had also been brought by humans). Nice try! But mongooses hunt during the daytime, while rats are active at night. So what's a hungry mongoose to do? Prey on birds, including the nene, a wild goose that is Hawaii's state bird. Once there were 25,000 nenes on Hawaii. Now, thanks to human interference, there are less than 500 nenes left in the wild.

Those nenes! They're just the thing when a mongoose gets the munchies.

From: "Big Mistakes!," *ASK* magazine, July/Aug 2003.

> Underline the native species named in the reading.

> Circle the species that were introduced by humans.

mongooses: small mammals that feed on other animals
prey on: eat
interference: changes

Look Back

What was the original problem faced by people in Hawaii? What solution did they find? What new problem did this solution create?

> **Complete the graphic organizer based on information from the reading.**

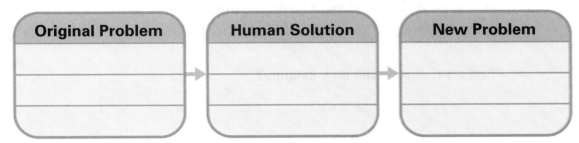

Original Problem	Human Solution	New Problem

Explore

STAYING BALANCED

In every ecosystem, there are animals that eat other animals for food. The animals that eat other animals are called **predators**. The animals that are eaten are called **prey**. The humans who brought the mongooses over to Hawaii were hoping that the animals would eat the rats as their prey.

Relationships between predators and prey within an ecosystem are balanced so that, normally, one group does not wipe out another group. But if a new species is introduced, the balance can be upset.

One of the reasons why predators don't wipe out prey is because the prey are often able to avoid predators. The ability to avoid predators is an adaptation that develops over thousands of years of living in the same area. It cannot be developed over just a couple of generations.

> **Why do you think the nenes are so easily hunted by the mongoose?**

Put It All Together

Look over the past pages. Think about what the kudzu story and the mongoose story have in common. In both cases, humans faced a problem with their local ecosystem.

> **What solution did the humans come up with in both cases?**

_____

_____

> **What went wrong with their solution?**

_____

_____

> **What can you conclude about introducing species into a new ecosystem?**

_____

_____

_____

Introduced species don't have to come from another country. Any species that is brought into an area where it doesn't normally live can cause problems.

Imagine that your friend Trisha is planning on setting her two pet goldfish free in a local pond where many native plants and animals live. Goldfish are not native to the pond ecosystem. In the space below, explain to Trisha why letting the fish go would not be a good idea. (Hint: What kinds of problems might the goldfish cause for native species?)

_____

_____

_____

_____

_____

UNIT 1: Life Science

What Did We Learn?

CHAPTER 1

What traits do scientists look at when classifying ladybugs?

_____

_____

CHAPTER 2

Why are a mole-rat's teeth so sensitive to touch?

_____

_____

_____

CHAPTER 3

Why are insect-eating plants often found in bogs?

_____

_____

_____

CHAPTER 4

What do the New Caledonian crow and the sea otter have in common?

_____

_____

CHAPTER 5

Why couldn't a dinosaur hatch out of a chicken egg?

_____

_____

CHAPTER 6

Why is it dangerous to bring plants and animals from one ecosystem to another?

_____

_____

UNIT 2: Earth Science

DID YOU KNOW?
Sometimes Earth's shadow falls on the moon. This event is called an eclipse of the moon.

Chapter 7
Earthquakes on the Edge
Find Out: Why do some places have so many earthquakes?

Chapter 8 Caverns Are Cool
Find Out: Can a stalactite grow in your lifetime?

Chapter 9 A Hiding Place
Find Out: Can you find a mesa by looking at a map?

Chapter 10
Caught in the Act?
Find Out: How did a dinosaur get named after something it didn't do?

Chapter 11 It's a Twister!
Find Out: Should you go home if a tornado is coming?

Chapter 12 Eclipsed!
Find Out: What shadow are you seeing during an eclipse of the moon?

Earthquakes on the Edge

Chapter 7

Have you ever experienced an earthquake?

If you have seen waves on an ocean or large lake, then you know what one kind of wave looks like. **Earthquakes** produce waves that pass through the earth instead of water. Usually when an earthquake wave passes, the ground shakes and so does everything on it. The shaking from an earthquake lasts only a few minutes. But while it is happening, the earthquake can cause a lot of changes to Earth's surface and anything that is on it.

What are the chances that you will experience an earthquake? It depends on where you live. In some parts of the world, every school has a plan for what to do in case of an earthquake. That's because they are common in those areas. In other places, a major earthquake is so rare that no person alive today has ever experienced one there. Where do earthquakes happen? Why do they happen in some places, but hardly ever in others?

In this chapter, you will read a description of what happens during an earthquake. Then you will find out why they happen more often in certain places.

Before You Read

Look around the room you are in. Imagine what would happen to the room and to the people and things in it if everything started shaking. Describe five specific changes that you can imagine happening in the room.

_____

_____

_____

_____

_____

SCIENCESAURUS
A STUDENT HANDBOOK
BLUE BOOK

Earth's Moving
Plates .... p. 176
Earthquakes
.... p. 180

SCiLINKS.
THE WORLD'S A CLICK AWAY

www.scilinks.org
Keyword:
Plate Tectonics
Code: GS5D040

Read

Moon Shadow, age 11, is a Chinese-American living in San Francisco, California in the early 1900s. Here, we see the great earthquake of 1906 through his eyes.

"The Earth Turns Fluid"

notes:

I had gotten dressed and gone out to the pump to get some water. The morning was filled with that soft, gentle twilight of spring, when everything is filled with soft, dreamy colors and shapes; so when the earthquake hit, I did not believe it at first. It seemed like a nightmare where everything you take to be the rock-hard, solid <u>basis</u> for reality becomes unreal.

Wood and stone and brick and the very earth became <u>fluidlike</u>. The pail beneath the pump jumped and rattled like a spider dancing on a hot stove. The ground <u>deliberately</u> seemed to slide right out from under me. I landed on my back hard enough to drive the wind from my lungs. The whole world had become unglued. Our stable and Miss Whitlaw's house and the <u>tenements</u> to either side <u>heaved</u> and <u>bobbed</u> up and down, riding the ground like ships on a heavy sea....

San Francisco before the earthquake

> <u>Underline</u> all the phrases on this page that tell how things moved during the earthquake.

basis: base, or foundation
fluidlike: like moving water
deliberately: on purpose

tenements: crowded apartment buildings
heaved: moved up and dow▮

San Francisco after the earthquake, April 18, 1906

Moon Shadow's father comes running out in bare feet. He has just enough time to say a few things to Moon Shadow and put on his shoes when something more happens...

[Father] started to get to his feet when the second <u>tremor</u> shook and he fell forward flat on his face. I heard the city bells ringing. They were rung by no human hand—the earthquake had just shaken them in their steeples. The second tremor was worse than the first. From all over came an <u>immense</u> wall of noise: of metal tearing, of bricks crashing, of wood breaking free from wood nails, and all. Everywhere, what man had built came undone. I was looking at a tenement house to our right and it just seemed to shudder and then collapse. One moment there were solid wooden walls and the next moment it had fallen with the cracking of wood and the tinkling of glass and the screams of people inside.

From: *Dragonwings* by Laurence Yep.

> <u>Underline</u> all the phrases on this page that tell how things moved during the second tremor.

bobbed: moved
tremor: earthquake wave
immense: huge

53

Look Back

The story is fictional but describes a real earthquake that took place in San Francisco, California on April 18, 1906. The reading describes the results of two different earthquake waves. Both waves were part of the same earthquake, but the second wave arrived a little while after the first.

> **The waves started out at the same place and at the same time. But they moved at different speeds. Which wave moved faster? How can you tell?**

Explore

TIMING EARTHQUAKE WAVES

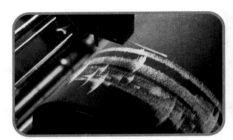

Vibrations show up as zigzag marks on a seismograph printout.

The shaking from an earthquake wave is very strong close to the place where the earthquake first occurs. As the wave travels away from the original location, the shaking in each new location that the wave passes gets less and less. People in places that are far away from the original location cannot even feel the earthquake wave that is passing. Scientists must use a machine called a **seismograph** to detect the tiny vibrations from far away earthquakes.

Scientists can use a seismograph to measure the amount of time that takes place between earthquake waves. They use this time to determine where the earthquake originally took place. The farther away the earthquake took place, the longer the amount of time between waves.

> **Imagine that a scientist in Denver measures the time in between two earthquake waves to be 3 minutes and 10 seconds. A scientist in San Diego measures the time in between waves to be 1 minute 50 seconds. Which scientist is closest to the place where the earthquake originally took place? Explain your answer.**

Explore

THE RING OF FIRE

Scientists can pinpoint exactly where an earthquake occurs using the data that they collect on earthquake waves. On the map below, the red dots show places where major earthquakes or volcanic eruptions have occurred.

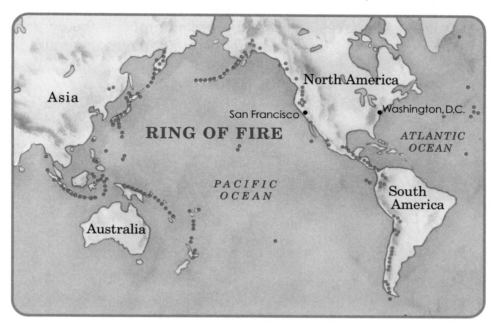

> **Are earthquakes just as common everywhere on Earth? Explain, using examples from the map.**

> **The land on the edges of the Pacific Ocean is sometimes called the Ring of Fire. Why do you think this area is given a special name?**

Explore

THE EDGES OF EARTH'S PLATES

Earth's surface, or crust, has huge cracks in it. The cracks divide the crust into large pieces, called **plates**. The whole crust is broken up into about ten major plates of different sizes. Even though you can't feel it, these plates are always moving. Sometimes the movement of these plates can cause earthquakes, which are more common at the edges of the plates. The map below shows some of the major plates that make up Earth's crust.

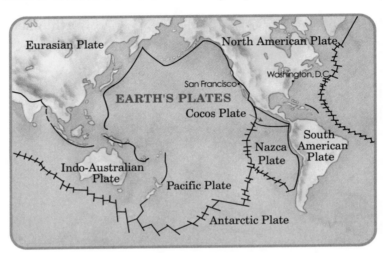

> Compare the map of Earth's plates with the map of the Ring of Fire on the previous page. Where does the Ring of Fire lie in relation to the plates?

> Why are earthquakes more common along the Ring of Fire than in other places?

> Find San Francisco and Washington, D.C. on the map. In which city do you think it's more common to have earthquakes? Explain your answer.

Caverns Are Cool

Chapter 8

What wonders lie down under?

Imagine that tomorrow is your big family reunion. To get ready, you go for a haircut. The next day, you see your family. An uncle who hasn't seen you in a year says, "Wow! You've grown taller!" But an aunt who sees you every weekend says, "Oh, you got your hair cut." Your aunt notices that your hair has been cut, because that was a sudden change. She hasn't noticed how much you've grown, because she sees you a lot, and growing taller is a slow change.

Some Earth events, like earthquakes, cause big changes very quickly—kind of like a hair cut, which changes how you look in just a few minutes. But other events take place so slowly that it is hard to see them happen—like the way that you grow taller, day by day.

In this chapter, you will explore how amazing rock formations are created in caverns underground. All it takes is the dripping of water and many thousands of years.

Before You Read

Close your eyes and think about caves. After one minute, open your eyes. On the lines below, write five or more words that describe the caves you imagine. In the box below, draw a small sketch of what you imagine when you think of a cave or cavern.

SCIENCESAURUS
A STUDENT HANDBOOK
BLUE BOOK

Weathering
.... p. 171
Erosion and
Deposition ... p. 172

SCI**LINKS.**
THE WORLD'S A CLICK AWAY

www.scilinks.org
Keyword: Caverns
Code: GS5D045

Read

In this newspaper article, Deborah Owen tells readers what to expect on a tour of Grand Caverns in Grottoes, Virginia.

"A Visit to Grand Caverns"

notes:

Grand Caverns might be called the granddaddy of <u>show caves</u>. Discovered in 1804, it's been open to the public continually since 1806, making it America's oldest show cave....*Parade Magazine* has rated Grand Caverns second only to Carlsbad Caverns in New Mexico.

...Caverns are cool—about 55 degrees [F] year-round. It's a good idea to take a sweater or jacket, and to wear comfortable walking shoes with good <u>traction</u>. The same dripping and seeping water that makes the stunning formations inside the caverns can make for slippery spots underfoot.

One of the first things our tour guide, Katie Brown, pointed out was that the formations extending down from the ceiling are called stalactites and the ones rising from the floor are stalagmites. They are formed by the <u>mineral deposits</u> in the water building up over long periods of time. It can take from 100 to 150 years to form one cubic inch of a stalactite.

> >Underline the words that describe what makes the cavern formations.

Stalactite ⎯⎯

Column ⎯⎯

Stalagmite ⎯⎯

show caves: caves or caverns with paid tours
traction: grip on slippery surfaces

mineral deposits: rock that was dissolved and then set down by water

Flowstone and draperies in Hurricane Crawl Cave, Sequoia National Park, California

Grand Caverns is known for having a large number of shield formations. Round and flat like a clamshell, shields have geologists <u>stumped</u> as to exactly how they are formed. Other types of formations typically found in caverns are columns, in which stalactites and stalagmites meet in the middle, <u>flowstone</u> and <u>draperies</u>. One unusual example we saw was in an area known as the Bridal Chamber. The Bridal Veil combines a shield formation with the rippling and <u>cascading</u> of flowstone and draperies.

...Brown entertained the youngsters on our tour with lighting tricks, ghost stories...and funny <u>anecdotes</u>....Don't be surprised if you work up an appetite on a cavern tour. It's good exercise, and many formations—a cheeseburger here, an ice cream cone there, a pizza hanging from the ceiling—resemble food.

From: *"In Grottoes' Grand Caverns; Form a Line for Stalactites, Stalagmites, Flowstone and Draperies"* by Deborah Owen, *Richmond (VA) Times-Dispatch*, August 14, 2003.

notes:

> <u>Underline</u> the type of formation that is still a mystery to scientists.

stumped: puzzled
flowstone: rock formation that looks like a frozen waterfall
draperies: rock formation that looks like hanging cloth
cascading: waterfall-like
anecdotes: stories

Look Back

The drawing at right shows what a cubic inch looks like.

> **How long does it take a cubic inch of stalactite to form?**

_____

> **About how many cubic inches could have been added to a stalactite since Grand Caverns first opened in 1806?**

_____

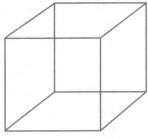

1 cubic inch

Activity

CREATING CAVERN FORMATIONS

Why do stalactites look like rock icicles?

What You Need:
- large bowl
- Epsom salts (about 250 mL, or 1 cup)
- warm water
- spoon
- 2 glass glasses or jars
- tray (to catch the extra solution)
- strip of cotton towel (about 1–2 cm wide and 45 cm long)
- 2 big paper clips (to weigh down the ends of the strip)
- small piece of paper towel

Cavern formations look like frozen water for a very good reason—they are made up of rock, but the rock is formed by water! First, water runs down through cracks in the limestone rock above the cavern. The water dissolves some of the rock along the way. Second, the water drips out of cracks in the cavern ceiling. Third, the water evaporates (turns from liquid to gas). The dissolved rock material is left behind as part of a new stalactite. In this activity, you will model two of these three steps.

What to Do:
1. Put the Epsom salts in the bowl. Add about 400 mL (1 to 2 cups) warm tap water. Stir with the spoon to dissolve the Epsom salts.
2. Place the two glasses on the tray about 30–40 centimeters apart. Pour half the liquid into each glass. *(continued on next page)*

(continued from previous page)

3. Put one paper clip on each end of the strip of towel. Put the strip into one of the glasses to get it soaking wet. Then pull it out again.

4. Put one end of the wet strip into each glass. Make sure each end is underwater. Let the strip hang down in the middle, between the two glasses. Make sure that the bottom part of the hanging strip is below the level of the liquid in the glasses.

5. Place a small piece of crumpled paper towel under the bottom part of the hanging strip where the dripping water falls.

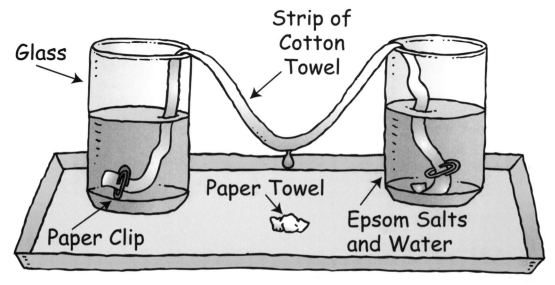

6. Observe the setup right away and then at the times listed in the table below. Record what you see each time in the second column. Use the words *stalactites*, *stalagmites*, and *columns*, if you see these features.

Time	Observation
immediately	
afternoon of day one	
morning of day two	
afternoon of day two	

61

Explore

ANALYZE A MODEL

There are three processes that take place in the making of cave formations. When the rock dissolves, that's called **weathering**. When the water takes the rock material with it, it's called **erosion**. When the water evaporates and leaves the rock material behind, it's called **deposition**.

> **In setting up your model of a cavern formation, you dissolved the Epsom salts in water. This is like the weathering of rock. Which part of the model is like erosion?**

_____

_____

_____

> **Look at your model of a cavern formation. Which part of the model is like deposition?**

_____

_____

_____

Science Journal

Look for examples of slow changes in your neighborhood over the next two weeks. How do permanent things change slowly over time? Slow changes include weathering, erosion, deposition, melting, and freezing. Copy the chart below onto a separate sheet of paper. Look for the kinds of examples suggested in the chart. An example is done for you.

Slow Change	Date and Place	What it looks like	What might have caused it
icicles forming or changing	February 10, edge of roof at home	long, bumpy spikes hanging down	snow melting and water freezing again
crack in paved road or sidewalk			
rut in dirt road			
garden soil washing away			
metal rusting			

How do you hide outside?

Imagine that your next-door neighbor is pounding on your door. She shouts that an enemy army is on the way! Everyone in the neighborhood has to go into hiding right now or be taken prisoner. Because there isn't much time, you need to hide somewhere nearby. Where would you go? What would you do?

Today, most North Americans are not used to events like this. Unfortunately, it is more common in some parts of the world. And, it has happened before in what is now the United States.

In this chapter, you will read part of a novel. It describes a village of Navajo, a Native American people, as they go into hiding. Their knowledge of the land near their home helps them to hide for a while. But it is impossible for them to hide forever.

Before You Read

Think about landforms in the place that you live. **Landforms** are features of Earth's surface. On the lines below, write three or more sentences that describe the shape of the land in and around your town. Are there any hills or mountains? Are there flat places? What does the shape of the land look like?

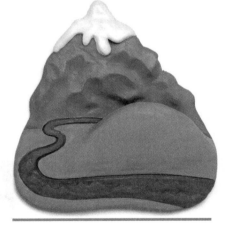

SCIENCE SAURUS
A STUDENT HANDBOOK
BLUE BOOK

Weathering ... p. 171
Erosion and
Deposition ... p. 172
Parts of a
Map .... p. 404

SCI LINKS.
THE WORLD'S A CLICK AWAY

www.scilinks.org
Keyword: Erosion
Code: GS5D050

Read

Bright Morning, a Navajo girl, is living in Canyon de Chelly [de SHAY], Arizona, in the 1860s. She tells how her people hid when soldiers came to drive them away.

"Up River, Uphill, into Hiding

notes:

> What did the people use for a trail when they first left the village? How did that help which way they went?

When the sun was high we <u>filed</u> out of the village and followed the river north, walking through the shallow water. At dusk we reached the trail that led upward to the south <u>mesa</u>....

The soldiers could not follow our path from the village because the flowing water covered our footsteps as fast as they were made. But when we moved out of the river our steps showed clear in the sand. After we were all on the trail some of the men broke branches from a tree and went back and swept away the marks we had left. There was no sign for the soldiers to see. They could not tell whether we had gone up the river or down.

The trail was narrow and steep. It was mostly slabs of stone which we scrambled over, lifting ourselves from one to the other. We crawled as much as we walked. In places the sheep had to

Canyon de Chelly

filed: walked in a long line   **mesa:** flat-topped land with cliffs at the edges

Navajo woman with her sheep, 1943

be carried and two of them slipped and fell into a <u>ravine</u>. The trail upward was less than half a mile long, but night was falling before we reached the end.

We made camp on the rim of the mesa, among rocks and <u>stunted</u> piñon trees. We did not think that the soldiers would come until morning, but we lighted no fires and ate a cold supper of corn-cakes. The moon rose and in a short time shone down into the <u>canyon</u>. It showed the river winding toward the south, past our peach orchards and <u>corrals</u> and <u>hogans</u>. Where the tall cliffs ended, where the river wound out of the canyon into the flatlands, the moon shone on white tents and <u>tethered</u> horses.

"The soldiers have come," my uncle said. "They will not look for us until morning. Lie down and sleep."

We made our beds among the rocks but few of us slept. At dawn we did not light fires, for fear the soldiers would see the rising smoke, and ate a cold breakfast. My father ordered everyone to gather stones and pile them where the trail entered the mesa. He posted a guard of young men at the trail head to use the stones if the soldiers came to attack us.

From: *Sing Down the Moon* by Scott O'Dell.

ravine: deep, narrow, valley
stunted: poorly-grown
canyon: steep-sided river valley

corrals: animal pens
hogans: houses
tethered: tied

notes:

> How do the people get ready to defend themselves against the soldiers?

> Where did Bright Morning's father expect the soldiers to attack from?

Look Back

> At first, the people in the story are walking in the river. Then they go up a trail to a mesa. What words and phrases in the reading describe the journey up this trail?

> Contrast the land the river flows through with the land leading up to the mesa. How are they different?

> What is the land at the top of the mesa like?

Explore

FORMATION OF LANDFORMS

Canyons and mesas are formed by weathering and erosion. **Weathering** is the wearing away of rock. **Erosion** is rock being worn away and moved to another place. Wind, water, and ice are the most common causes of weathering and erosion.

> What do you think was the cause of the weathering and erosion that formed the canyons and mesas in the area described in the reading?

> Look at the picture of the mesa below. Mesa is the Spanish word for "table." Why do you think that mesas have this name?

Explore

A **relief map** shows features of the land, such as hills and valleys, by showing the shadows that they cast. The shaded areas give you an idea of about how tall or how deep a feature is. For example, the pictures below show how a river, a canyon, and a mesa might appear on a relief map.

River

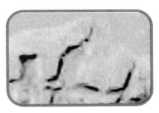
Canyon

Mesa

> The relief map below shows Canyon de Chelly. Look closely at the map. Find one example of a river, a canyon, and a mesa. Then, label each feature with its name (River, Canyon, Mesa).

> Compare the relief map to the description of where the people in the reading traveled. The reading said that they walked north along a river and then hiked up a steep cliff wall to the top of a mesa. Use a pencil to draw one possible route that the characters could have taken.

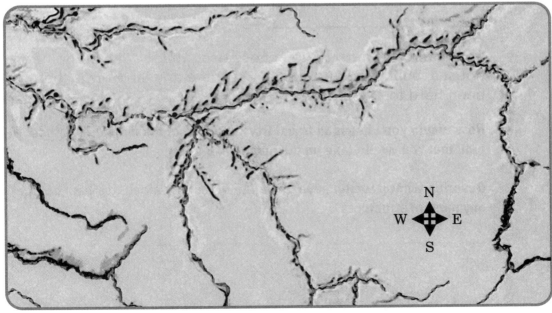

Relief map of Canyon de Chelly

Project

THE LANDFORMS IN YOUR AREA

Your teacher will provide you with a relief map of your area. Look at the map. Can you find where your school is located on the map? Can you find your neighborhood? Choose a small area on the map that has at least one interesting landform, such as a mountain, hill, flatland, canyon, river valley, mesa, or cliff. Sketch that area of the map in the box below. Label any interesting landforms that you see.

Imagine what the area you chose used to look like before there were houses, buildings, and roads. Are there any landforms that would have been hard to climb or cross?

> **How would you choose to travel from one side of the map to the other? Draw the path that you would take on the map above.**

> **Describe what it would have been like to journey along this path before there were any modern structures.**

For every observation, there can be many explanations!

Imagine this: Your little brother leaves toys all over the yard. He says that if you pick them up, he'll give you his allowance and take out the trash for you. So you start picking them up. Your mother sees you and says, "What are you doing playing with your brother's toys? You don't let him play with yours!" Of course, you can explain what you were doing. But what if you couldn't? What if you were suddenly buried by a sandstorm at that exact moment? You and the toys are trapped, and you all become fossils in a rock. Millions of years from now, what would people think you were *really* doing?

Scientists try to figure out puzzles like this all the time. They use the best information that they have to explain what they see. But in science, new discoveries can change old explanations.

In this chapter, you will learn about a famous fossil find—the discovery of fossil dinosaur eggs! Next to the eggs lay a fossil of a mysterious new dinosaur. What was it doing there?

Before You Read

Think about a time when you *thought* you saw or heard someone doing something, but it turned out they were really doing something else. What made you believe they were doing something other than what they were really doing? Why did you think that?

_____

_____

_____

_____

SCIENCESAURUS
A STUDENT HANDBOOK
BLUE BOOK

Making Scientific Observations
.... p. 11
Making Inferences ..... p. 18
Fossils .... p. 185

SCI LINKS.
THE WORLD'S A CLICK AWAY

www.scilinks.org
Keyword: Fossils
Code: GS5D055

Read

The Gobi is a huge desert in central Asia. It was there, in 1923, that fossils of dinosaur eggs were discovered by scientists, including George Olsen and Roy Chapman Andrews.

"In the Gobi, 1923"

notes:

At first sight, Andrews thought the dinosaur eggs looked like [rock formations] or maybe bird eggs. ...But judging by the shape, size, and crinkled texture of the eggs, the scientists were quite sure they were dinosaur eggs. They also agreed that the eggs probably belonged to *Protoceratops* because these small dinosaurs were so common.

As Olsen continued to scrape away sand and loose rock around the nest, he uncovered parts of a skeleton of a small, clawed dinosaur a few inches from the eggs. From the position of the bones, it looked as though this dinosaur had been buried by a sudden sandstorm just as it was about to rob the eggs from the nest....

Back in the laboratory..., Dr. Osborn...agreed with the scientists on the <u>expedition</u> that [the fossil eggs] must be from *Protoceratops*. His decision, like theirs, was based on little more than the <u>abundance</u> of these dinosaurs at the site.

[He also] agreed that [the dinosaur found near the eggs] probably had been...robbing the nest. Osborn gave that ostrich-size dinosaur the scientific name *Oviraptor*.... *Ovi* means "egg," raptor means "robber...."

> <u>Underline</u> the name of the dinosaur that probably laid the eggs.

> (Circle) the name of the dinosaur found near the eggs.

From: *Tracking Dinosaurs in the Gobi*, by Margery Facklam.

expedition: trip

abundance: large number

Protoceratops

Explore

An **observation** is something that you note using your senses. Everybody who makes the observation generally agrees about it, because there is no guessing about what they see, touch, hear, or smell.

> **What observations led the scientists to believe the fossil eggs were dinosaur eggs?**

_____

_____

An **inference** is an idea that explains an observation or answers a question. An inference is based on an observation. Often, more than one inference can be made for the same observations. The scientists in 1923 made some inferences about the eggs and about the dinosaurs. Fill in the chart below, based on the reading.

Question	Inference	Observation that the inference was based on
Which kind of dinosaur laid the eggs?		
What was the *Oviraptor* dinosaur doing near the eggs?		

71

Read

Seventy years later, a new group of scientists discovered more fossil dinosaurs and eggs in the same desert.

"In the Gobi, 1993"

notes:

> How were the new fossil eggs like the ones found in 1923?

> How was the fossil egg Mark Norell found different from the others?

After lunch that first day, Mark Norell found a <u>concentration</u> of dinosaur eggs and nests. ...[H]e saw one that had broken open, <u>revealing</u> the tiny bones of an <u>embryo</u> dinosaur. The seven-inch-long egg was oval shaped, and its surface was crinkled—the same kind of egg George Olsen had found at the Flaming Cliffs seventy years before. These were just like the eggs from the dinosaur named *Protoceratops*. But no one had ever seen [a complete] embryo in one of those eggs.

...Each new find seemed more exciting than the last, but one discovery sent a shock through the camp. Luis Chiappe and Amy Davidson were chipping away at an *Oviraptor* skeleton when they found eggs under it. They knew immediately that it was a major scientific discovery, but they had to wait until they could examine it in the lab before they made an announcement. ...

During the winter of 1993–1994, Davidson spent more than four hundred hours cleaning the bones of the tiny embryo in its eggshell. The seventy-year-old mistake was finally corrected. The embryo was not *Protoceratops*, but an *Oviraptor*. The *Oviraptor* found in 1923 at the Flaming Cliffs was not an egg robber. She was probably protecting her own nest.

From: *Tracking Dinosaurs in the Gobi*, by Margery Facklam.

concentration: large number in a small area
revealing: showing

embryo: body of an unhatched animal

Look Back

> What made the fossil eggs found in 1993 more useful to the scientists than the fossil eggs found in 1923?

Oviraptor

Explore

HOW A FOSSIL FORMS

When a dead animal is buried, the soft parts of its body decay leaving the hard parts, such as the bones and teeth. These hard parts can become fossils over very long periods of time. Water carrying dissolved minerals slowly replaces the bone material with the minerals, making a rock shaped exactly like the bone material. This rock is a fossil. The hard shells of eggs can also become fossils by this process.

If the embryo inside an egg has a hard skeleton, it too can become a fossil.

> What part of the adult *Oviraptor* became a fossil?

> What parts of the eggs described in the readings became fossils?

An Oviraptor embryo.

Explore

NEW OBSERVATIONS, NEW INFERENCES

The scientists in 1993 and 1994 made some observations and inferences about the fossil eggs and dinosaurs they found. Fill in the chart below, based on the second reading.

Question	Inference	Observation that the inference was based on
Which kind of dinosaur laid the eggs?		
What was the *Oviraptor* dinosaur doing near the eggs?		

Put It All Together

> **Look back over the past few pages. What information about the fossil eggs did the scientists have in 1993 that the scientists in 1923 did not have?**

> **How did this new information change the identification of the fossil eggs?**

> **How did the inference made about the *Oviraptor* change from 1923 to 1993?**

It's a Twister!

Chapter 11

You've seen clouds shaped like many different things, but what about a cloud shaped like a spinning funnel?

A gentle breeze is a pleasant part of a spring day. But spring can also bring fierce storms called **tornadoes**. A tornado is a funnel-shaped storm cloud caused by rotating, high-speed winds. The winds have such high speeds that they can cause serious damage to buildings and property. Tornadoes can happen anywhere, at any time of the year. But in some parts of the country, they are most common in the spring.

In this chapter, you will read about a tornado that raged through a town on an April afternoon. You will also make a model of a tornado and figure out the safest place for you to go if a tornado has been seen in your area.

Before You Read

Think about the wind where you live. Is it always windy? What is the wind usually like? What is it like on a very windy day? How strong does wind have to be to pick something up and move it? Describe at least three different winds you have observed. Include the strongest wind you have ever experienced.

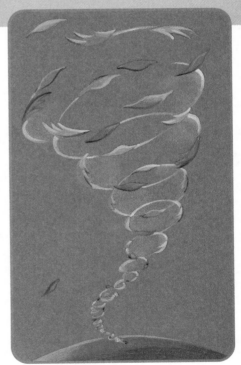

Tornadoes ... p. 213
A STUDENT HANDBOOK
BLUE BOOK

www.scilinks.org
Keyword:
Tornadoes
Code: GS5D060

Read

Xenia, Ohio was one of many towns hit hard during a huge outbreak of tornadoes on the afternoon of April 3, 1974.

"No School Tomorrow"

notes:

...Of the town's twelve schools, six <u>sustained</u> severe damage or were <u>reduced to rubble</u>. Fortunately, most of the students had already left for the day, but not all.

Ruth Venuti, 18, was waiting at Xenia High School for a friend to give her a ride home. In the distance she noticed an <u>immense</u> black cloud change into a gigantic, rotating funnel. Ruth realized a tornado was headed her way. She raced to the auditorium to <u>alert</u> drama club members rehearsing for an upcoming performance of *The Boyfriend.* Bursting in on the rehearsal, Ruth asked if anybody wanted to see a tornado.

> <u>Underline</u> the sentence that describes the tornado forming.

A tornado is a huge funnel-shaped cloud.

sustained: experienced
reduced to rubble: smashed into small pieces

immense: huge
alert: tell about a risk

Mossy Grove, Tennessee, after a tornado, 2002

David Heath, an English teacher and the club's director, jumped off the stage and told the students to follow. They dashed to the hallway, where through the windows they <u>spied</u> an enormous funnel <u>writhing</u> just 200 feet (61 m) away. Terrified, the group took cover in the school's central corridor. Seconds later the tornado struck. For four minutes, mud, wood, dirt, broken glass, and other chunks of <u>debris</u> swirled above the students, who were now lying on the floor.

None of the students were killed or seriously injured. But the twister had <u>obliterated</u> the top floor of the school and partially caved in the auditorium roof. <u>Sprawled</u> across the stage where students had rehearsed only minutes earlier was an upside-down school bus.

From: *Nature's Fury: Eyewitness Reports of Natural Disasters,*
by Carole G. Vogel.

> How long was the tornado over the school?

> How did the tornado change the school during that time?

spied: saw
writhing: twisting
debris: broken pieces

obliterated: completely destroyed
sprawled: spread out

Look Back

Some weather events build up slowly. Others build up very quickly. A tornado forms when a thunderstorm meets cool winds high in the atmosphere. The winds cause a rapid, spinning cloud movement in the thunderstorm. Under certain conditions, tornadoes can develop suddenly and move very quickly.

> **Do you think the tornado in the reading built up slowly or quickly? Give examples from the reading to explain your answer.**

_____

_____

_____

_____

Activity

BOTTLED TWISTER

How does a tornado move things?

What You Need:
- $^1/_2$ liter (20-oz) plastic bottle with straight sides
- cap for the bottle
- water
- 2 or 3 drops dish soap
- pinch of glitter
- 2 or 3 pieces aquarium gravel

A tornado is a kind of vortex. A **vortex** is a swirling, twirling, moving shape in water or air. It takes energy to get a vortex started. But once it's started, it can keep going for awhile before it slows down. In this activity, you will make a vortex in a bottle. Then you will observe how the motion of a vortex can move things that are caught in it.

What to Do:
1. Fill the bottle most of the way with water. Add 2 or 3 drops of dish soap. Do not add more than 2 or 3 drops! If you do, empty the bottle, rinse it, and start over again.
2. Add a pinch of glitter and two or three bits of gravel.

(continued on next page)

(continued from previous page)

3. Put the cap on the bottle. Seal it tightly!

4. Hold the bottle sideways in both hands so that the length of the bottle is parallel to the ground. Move the bottle so it makes circles in the air, as shown in the picture on the left. Move it fast! Do this for 10–15 seconds, then IMMEDIATELY turn the bottle upside-down, as shown in the picture on the right. Watch what happens inside the bottle.

Move the bottle in a circle.

Quickly turn bottle upside-down.

NOTE: Making the vortex takes practice. Be patient and keep trying. A common mistake is moving the bottle in a bigger circle at one end than the other. Another common mistake is turning the bottle in your hands as if it were rolling. Hold the bottle sideways, and move your arms quickly to make circles in the air.

> **Describe what is happening in the bottle.**

> **Make the vortex again. Describe what the gravel pieces do.**

> **How is the vortex in the bottle like a tornado? How is it different?**

Science Journal

In the reading, the student asked if anybody wanted to see the tornado. But you should never try to watch a tornado. Instead you should quickly find a safe place to stay until the tornado is gone. During a tornado, the strong winds can cause windows to shatter, objects to fly about at high speeds, and walls and roofs to be torn apart or collapse. To avoid being hurt by these things, follow this list of tornado safety tips.

Tornado Safety

- Get out of cars, buses, and other vehicles. If you cannot find shelter, lie flat in a ditch or underneath an overpass and cover your head.
- Go indoors and into the basement. If there is no basement, go to the lowest floor.
- Go to a room or hallway near the middle of the building. It should have no outside walls, windows, or skylights. Bathrooms are often a good choice.
- Avoid cafeterias, gymnasiums, and auditoriums. Most are unsafe during a tornado.
- Lie face–down and cover your head with your arms.

Source: National Weather Service Web Site

> **Look back at the reading. Where did the students go when the tornado arrived? Was this a good place to go, according to the safety information above?**

> **Think about your school. What is the safest place to go if a tornado is coming? Explain why that place is safest.**

> **Think about your home. What is the safest place to go there if a tornado is coming? Explain why that place is safest.**

Eclipsed!

Chapter 12

What happens when the moon is eclipsed?

Imagine yourself at a movie theater. A person stands up to go for popcorn. The light from the projector hits the person, and the person's shadow is seen on the screen. Please move out of the way! That area of the screen is dark until the person moves away.

When the person's shadow is seen on the screen, it is kind of like what happens during an **eclipse**. What is an eclipse? It's a shadow passing across an object in space. In an eclipse of the moon, the moon moves through Earth's shadow. There is a shadow because light from the sun is blocked by Earth. The light that would normally make the moon appear bright in the night sky doesn't reach the moon during the eclipse.

In this chapter, you will learn what to expect during an eclipse of the moon. You'll also find out one reason that eclipses are important to scientists.

Before You Read

What do you imagine an eclipse looks like? An eclipse of the moon happens at night. If you have seen an eclipse of the moon, describe what you saw. If not, describe what you imagine an eclipse of the moon would look like.

SCLINKS.
THE WORLD'S A CLICK AWAY

www.scilinks.org
Keyword: Eclipses
Code: GS5D065

Read

Ira Flatow hosts a radio show called "Science Friday." In this transcript, he talks with scientist Derrick Pitts about an upcoming eclipse of the moon.

"A Lunar Eclipse"

notes:

> Did astronomers really plan the eclipse?

> Underline when a lunar eclipse happens.

During a lunar eclipse, the moon appears red.

IRA FLATOW, host: [W]e're going to talk about <u>astronomy</u> because tomorrow is International Astronomy Day. ... And to help celebrate that event, astronomers have <u>arranged for</u> a <u>lunar eclipse</u> later in the week. Isn't that something? OK. Now they didn't exactly arrange for the eclipse, but they can help us figure out when to look for it .... Joining me to talk more about it...is Derrick Pitts. He's the chief astronomer for The Franklin Institute in Philadelphia. ...Welcome back to SCIENCE FRIDAY, Derrick.

DERRICK PITTS: Thank you very much, Ira. It's great to be here.

FLATOW: First, tell everybody what this kind of eclipse is....

PITTS: ...[T]his is a lunar eclipse.... The lunar eclipse happens at full moon <u>phase</u>. So in this part of the world, everyone, as long as the sky is clear, will be able to see the moon as it is full, and they'll be able to watch and see as the moon starts to change color. And in this particular instance, it's going to develop into a very deep, rich red.

FLATOW: So it's not going to go away; it's just going to get dark red, and you can see it....

PITTS: You'll be able to see it without any problem at all.

From: *Talk of the Nation: Science Friday*, May 9, 2003, second hour, National Public Radio.

astronomy: study of stars, planets, moons, and other things in space

arranged for: planned
lunar eclipse: eclipse of the moon
phase: stage, or time period

Explore

THE MOON AS A MOTORCYCLE

In the pictures below, a motorcycle is passing a truck on the road at sun rise. The sun is shining from the right (East). In the first box, the shadows of the motorcycle and truck fall to the left (West), away from the sun.

> **Shade in the shadows of the truck and the motorcycle in the other two pictures.**

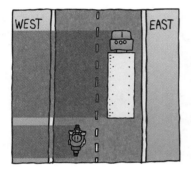  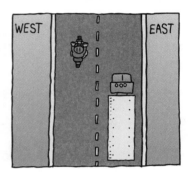

In the pictures below, the moon is traveling in its orbit around Earth. The sun is shining from the right. The first box shows the shadows of the moon and Earth, which point away from the sun. (They are not to scale.)

> **Shade in the shadows of Earth and the moon in the other two pictures.**

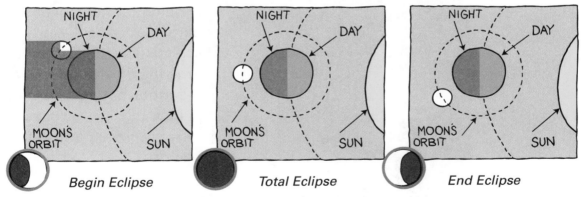

Begin Eclipse   Total Eclipse   End Eclipse

> **Compare both sets of pictures. What happens to both the motorcycle and the moon?**

_____

_____

_____

⌐Read

Lunar eclipses are more than just fun to watch. They're also useful. Flatow and Pitts talk about how lunar eclipses help scientists observe motions of Earth and the moon.

"Timing Earth's Shadow"

notes:

_____

_____

_____

_____

>Underline what the scientists use to time Earth's motion and the moon's motion.

FLATOW: Now getting back to the lunar eclipse, we don't need any special equipment to look at the moon here—Right?—and see the eclipse.

PITTS: No, you don't.

FLATOW: But if you have a small telescope or a pair of binoculars, is it fun to watch the shadow move across the moon if you can look at the moon a little closer?

PITTS: You sure can. And it is fun to watch the shadow move across because if you wanted to, you could actually watch it as it passes over specific craters. There are <u>crater timings</u> that you

can look for on the Web that will tell you when the shadow is going to move over particular craters. And scientists actually use this to time the Earth's motion and the moon's motion, by looking at how quickly the shadow moves across particular craters....

From: *Talk of the Nation: Science Friday*, May 9, 2003, second hour, National Public Radio.

crater timings: times that the edge of Earth's shadow will pass across certain craters

Explore

These three photos were taken in Iceland during a lunar eclipse in January, 2001.

7:00 P.M.

7:16 P.M.

7:32 P.M.

> **How much time passed between the first and the second photo?** _____

> **Between the second and the third?** _____

> **Between the first and the third?** _____

> **How does the shadow on the moon change from one photo to the next?**

_____

_____

Look at the first photo. Arrows are pointing to two dark, round areas on the moon's surface.

> **Look for the same two dark areas in the second photo. What happened to the dark areas and the shadow of Earth between the first and second photos?**

_____

> **Look at the third photo. Where are the dark areas now?**

_____

> **Find the dark area near the edge of the moon in the third photo. Predict how long it will take for the shadow to cover that area.**

_____

Put It All Together

Look back at the truck and motorcycle pictures on page 83. On each picture, draw a *tiny* bug on the shady side of the truck.

Imagine that you are the bug riding on the shady side of the truck. You are so small, and the truck is so big, that you can't tell that the truck is moving. (Pretend you can't feel the wind.) But you can tell that the motorcycle is moving. You watch the motorcycle turn dark as it goes into the shadow of the truck. You watch it pass in the shadow. Then you watch it become light again as it moves back into the sunshine.

> **How can the changes from light to dark to light again help you see how fast the motorcycle is moving past the truck? (Hint: Think about how quickly the light-dark-light change happens if the motorcycle moves quickly. Does the change happen as quickly when the motorcycle moves slowly?)**

> **Now compare the bug on the truck to a person watching an eclipse while standing on the shady side of Earth—the part of Earth where it is night. How is the bug watching the motorcycle like a person watching the eclipse?**

UNIT 2: Earth Science

What Did We Learn?

CHAPTER 7

What causes so many earthquakes along the Ring of Fire?

_____

_____

_____

_____

CHAPTER 8

Why can't a stalactite form in your lifetime?

_____

_____

_____

CHAPTER 9

How do rivers form canyons and mesas?

_____

_____

_____

CHAPTER 10

How did the dinosaur *Oviraptor* get the wrong name? What happened to correct the scientists' mistake?

_____

_____

_____

CHAPTER 11

Why shouldn't you go home if you see a tornado? What should you do instead?

_____

_____

_____

CHAPTER 12

What do scientists use Earth's shadow for during a lunar eclipse?

_____

_____

UNIT 3: Physical Science

DID YOU KNOW?
Some frogs have poisons on their skins that help defend them from animals that want to eat them

Chapter 13 Frog Chemist
Find Out: How does a frog use chemicals to protect itself?

Chapter 14 Secret Messages
Find Out: Why do spies need to know about chemicals?

Chapter 15 Electricity Bike
Find Out: How can you use your bike to blend up a tasty smoothie?

Chapter 16 Magic Machine?
Find Out: What do all machines need in order to run?

Chapter 17
Desert Refrigerator
Find Out: How can you keep food cool in the middle of the desert?

Chapter 18 Light Tricks
Find Out: How can light trick your eye?

Who would want to eat poisonous insects?

What do you think of when you hear the word "chemical"? Do you think of a person in a white coat with glasses and test tubes full of purple liquid? The purple liquid would be a chemical, but so are the plastic in the glasses and the fabric in the white coat. Actually, everything around you is made up of chemicals—your desk, the floor, the light bulb above your head, and even your own body.

When people say "chemicals," they usually mean chemical compounds. A **chemical compound** is a substance made up of two or more **elements** that are chemically joined. An element is the most basic kind of matter. Oxygen is an element. Water, which is made up of oxygen and hydrogen, is a chemical compound.

In this chapter, you will learn about an animal that makes a special kind of chemical compound, one that helps protect it from other animals. You will also learn how to identify chemical compounds based on their abilities to change when they meet other chemical compounds.

Before You Read

Can you think of any animals that use a chemical compound to attack other animals or to protect themselves? For example, some stinging insects inject their victims with a venom, which is a chemical compound. List at least four animals that are poisonous or that can sting other animals.

SCIENCESAURUS
A STUDENT HANDBOOK
BLUE BOOK

Physical and Chemical Properties ... p. 246
Elements ..... p. 250
Compounds p. 256

SCILINKS.
THE WORLD'S A CLICK AWAY

www.scilinks.org
Keyword:
Chemical Properties of Matter
Code: GS5D070

Read

Scientists have been wondering how poisonous frogs are able to make their poisons. Here's what the scientists found out.

"Poison Frog"

notes:

Talk about playing with your food.

Scientists have discovered a poisonous frog that takes up a <u>toxin</u> from its food and makes the chemical even deadlier. It's the first example of a frog using <u>chemistry</u> to make a poison for its own <u>defense</u> stronger.

Several types of frogs from South America, Australia, and Madagascar carry deadly poisons in their skin. When raised in zoos and <u>aquariums</u>, however, most of the frogs grow up to be totally harmless.

About 10 years ago, researchers… figured out that many <u>poison dart frogs</u> take up toxins from the food they eat, including

> <u>Underline</u> the words that describe what happens to most of the poisonous frogs raised in zoos and aquariums.

toxin: poison
chemistry: the science of elements and chemical compounds
defense: protection

aquariums: a kind of zoo for plants and animals that live in water
poison dart frogs: a group of frogs that all produce poisons

Dendrobates auratus is only about 4 centimeters long, but it can still defend itself.

ants and other insects. If such <u>prey</u> isn't available, the frogs get no toxins to store in their skins.

Scientists later found out that the frogs weren't just storing the toxin in their skin. They were also improving it....

More recently, scientists were working with a toxin...often found on the skin of the...green poison dart frog *(Dendrobates auratus).* The scientists sprinkled the toxin on termites and fruit flies, which they then fed to the <u>captive</u> [poison dart] frogs.

Later <u>analyses</u> of the frogs' skins showed that about 80 percent of the [toxin] had been <u>converted</u> to a different toxin.... The new toxin was five times more poisonous to mice than the original chemical.

Scientists were surprised by their findings. Any creature that tries to eat a wild *Dendrobates* would get an even bigger surprise. It's quite possible that its frog-leg dinner would be its last!

From: "Frog Chemist Creates a Deadlier Poison." *Science News for Kids,* Sept 10, 2003.

notes:

> How was the new toxin different from the original toxin?

prey: an animal that is eaten for food
captive: caged

analyses: studies
converted: changed

Look Back

The reading describes a lab experiment with green poison dart frogs and insects sprinkled with a toxin. The experiment demonstrates what happens in the wild with the poison dart frogs and the toxic insects they normally eat.

> Look at the chart below, which shows the poison dart frogs in three different situations. Decide whether the frog is poisonous or not poisonous and (circle) the correct word. Look back at the reading to help you.

Frogs in the wild that eat wild insects	Frogs in the lab that eat normal insects	Frogs in the lab that eat insects sprinkled with toxin
Poisonous or Not Poisonous?	Poisonous or Not Poisonous?	Poisonous or Not Poisonous?

> What can you conclude about how the frogs in the lab get the toxins in their skins?

> What can you conclude about how the frogs in the wild get the toxins in their skins?

> Why didn't the frogs raised in zoos and aquariums have toxins in their skins?

Explore

The world is made up of many different kinds of chemical compounds. Different compounds contain different combinations of elements. These elements give each compound its own unique set of chemical properties. **Chemical properties** describe the ability of a chemical compound to react with other compounds.

How can you determine the chemical properties of a compound? By seeing how it reacts with other compounds. For example, you can see how a chemical compound affects an animal when it interacts with the compounds found in the animal's own body.

Look back at the reading. The original toxin sprinkled on the frog's food was changed by the frog's body into a new toxin found on the frog's skin.

> **Think about how the two different toxins affected the mice. How were the chemical properties of the new toxin found on the frog's skin different from the chemical properties of the original toxin?**

Activity

OBSERVING CHEMICAL PROPERTIES

Can you identify a chemical property?

What You Need:

- 4 small paper cups
- 2 tablespoons purple cabbage juice
- $\frac{1}{2}$ teaspoon baking soda
- $\frac{1}{2}$ teaspoon cream of tartar
- 2 tablespoons vinegar

If you see a change in the appearance of chemical compounds when they are added together, you might be observing a chemical property of those compounds. Try it out in this activity. *(continued on next page)*

(continued from previous page)

What to Do:

1. Label four paper cups 1–4.
2. Put 1 tablespoon of purple cabbage juice into cups 1 and 2.
3. To cup 1, add $\frac{1}{4}$ teaspoon of baking soda. To cup 2, add $\frac{1}{4}$ teaspoon of cream of tartar.
4. What happens in cups 1 and 2? Write your observations in the chart.
5. Put 1 tablespoon of vinegar into cups 3 and 4.
6. To cup 3, add $\frac{1}{4}$ teaspoon of baking soda. To cup 4, add $\frac{1}{4}$ teaspoon of cream of tartar.
7. What happens in cups 3 and 4? Write your observations in the chart.

What Do You See?

Cup	Liquid	Powder	Observation
1	Purple cabbage juice	Baking soda	
2	Purple cabbage juice	Cream of tartar	
3	Vinegar	Baking soda	
4	Vinegar	Cream of tartar	

When baking soda is mixed with purple cabbage juice, the liquid changes color. That's because a chemical property of baking soda is that it turns purple cabbage juice green.

> **What is another chemical property of baking soda?**

_____

_____

> **What is a chemical property of cream of tartar?**

_____

_____

Sometimes, you need to send a message that no one else can read.

Imagine that you are away at summer camp. You want to write to your parents and tell them how homesick you are. You don't want anyone else to find out. Unfortunately, the camp counselors read all the letters you write before they go in the mail. How can you get a secret message to your parents? Why not use invisible ink?

Invisible inks are inks that cannot be seen when they are written or after they have dried. Only the person who sent the message and the person who is supposed to read the message know how to make the ink visible and uncover the message. In this chapter, you'll read about different kinds of chemicals that are used as invisible inks. Then, you'll use what you learned to create your own secret messages.

Before You Read

Spies have been using invisible ink to send secret messages for hundreds of years. Look at the picture at right. It shows a letter written by an American spy during the Revolutionary War. In between the lines of the ordinary letter is a secret message that the spy wrote using invisible ink. You can see now that the message has been uncovered and looks very dark. Whoever received the letter knew what to do to the paper to reveal the message hidden between the lines.

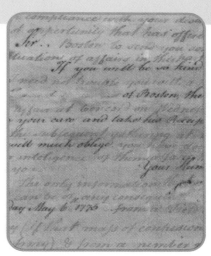

A letter written by Benjamin Thompson on May 6th, 1775

> **Why do you think the spy wrote the secret message between the lines of an ordinary letter?**

_____

_____

_____

_____

SCIENCESAURUS
A STUDENT HANDBOOK
BLUE BOOK

Physical and Chemical Properties ... p. 246
Chemical Changes ...... p. 266

SC LINKS.
THE WORLD'S A CLICK AWAY

www.scilinks.org
Keyword:
Chemical Changes
Code: GS5D075

Read

Jimmy and his friend The Bug are characters in a magazine column. They answer questions about science and nature. In this issue, they answer a question about invisible ink. How does invisible ink work?

"Invisible Ink"

notes:

Secret writing is very old and there are lots of invisible ink recipes. These inks work in different ways to hide and <u>reveal</u> messages written with them.

Some invisible inks—like milk, vinegar, or lemon juice—darken when they're heated. You can read messages written with them because they burn faster than the paper they're written on.

Other secret inks are <u>solutions</u> of chemicals that are colorless when dry but become visible when <u>treated</u> with another chemical, called a <u>reagent</u>.

Messages can even be written inside eggs, using a mixture of vinegar and a chemical called alum. Messages written with this ink are <u>absorbed</u> through the shell. When the egg is boiled and peeled, the message appears [on the boiled egg].

> Why do you think the inks described in the reading look "invisible" on paper?

reveal: show
solutions: liquid mixtures
treated: combined

reagent: a chemical that causes another chemical to change
absorbed: soaked up

From: "Jimmy + The Bug," *ASK* magazine, Jan/Feb 2003.

Look Back

> There were two types of secret inks described in the reading. Fill in the diagram below to compare the two types of ink and how they change.

Secret Ink: Milk, vinegar, or lemon juice

Secret Ink: Solutions that can be treated with a chemical

What does it look like when it is dry?

What does it look like when it is dry?

How do you change the ink to reveal it?

How do you change the ink to reveal it?

How does the ink change?

How does the ink change?

Explore

CHANGES IN MATTER

Invisible inks go through a chemical change when they are made visible. What is a chemical change? Wood burning, an old bike rusting, bread baking in the oven—all these are examples of chemical changes. A **chemical change** happens when two or more chemicals combine to produce new chemicals. The new chemicals might have different colors, textures, or smells than the original chemicals. These differences can be clues that a chemical change has taken place.

> Look back at diagram you just completed above. What clue tells you that a chemical change has taken place when invisible ink is revealed?

Activity

INVISIBLE INK #1

What's the recipe for invisible ink?

What You Need:

- lemon juice
- cotton swabs or toothpicks
- white paper
- lamp

What To Do:

1. Dip the cotton swab or toothpick in the lemon juice.
2. Use the wet cotton swab or toothpick to write a secret message on a piece of white paper.
3. Let the paper dry for 15 minutes. You should not be able to see the message.
4. Once the message is dry, exchange secret message papers with a friend.
5. Turn the lamp on.
6. Carefully hold your friend's paper near the warm light bulb for several minutes.

> **Can you read the secret message? What does it say?**

> **What evidence, or clue, tells you that a chemical change has taken place?**

> **What caused the chemical change to take place?**

> **Look back at the reading. What other inks besides lemon juice could be used in this activity?**

Activity

INVISIBLE INK #2

Can you make another kind of invisible ink?

What You Need:

- baking soda mixed with water
- purple grape juice
- cotton swabs or toothpicks
- cotton balls
- white paper

What To Do:

1. Dip the cotton swab or toothpick in the baking soda solution.
2. Use the wet cotton swab or toothpick to write a secret message on a piece of white paper.
3. Let the paper dry for 15 minutes. You should not be able to see the message.
4. Once the message is dry, exchange secret message papers with a friend.
5. Dip a cotton ball in grape juice.
6. Gently rub the wet cotton ball all over the paper.

> **Can you read the secret message? What does it say?**

> **What evidence, or clue, tells you that a chemical change has taken place?**

> **What caused the chemical change to take place?**

> **Look back at the reading. Which of the two types of inks did you use in this activity**

Chapter 15

How can a bike make electricity?

Most homes in the Unites States have electricity. This electricity is used to run all sorts of useful machines and fun toys. But not everyone around the world is so lucky. In many places—especially those that are far away from big cities—people don't even have electricity to light their homes.

Electricity is a form of energy. It is also called electrical energy. Electricity is produced from other forms of energy. For example, the heat energy given off by burning coal can be changed into electricity. So can the energy of motion from wind or moving water. In this chapter, you will read about a student in South America who came up with a very original way to produce electricity.

Before You Read

There are many ways to produce electricity. There are even more ways to use electricity. How is electricity used in your home?

> **List at least six ways that electricity is used in your home.**

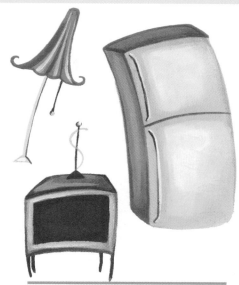

SCIENCESAURUS
A STUDENT HANDBOOK
BLUE BOOK

Forms of
Energy .... p. 285
Energy
Changes ..... p. 286
Electricity ... p. 296

SCI LINKS.
THE WORLD'S A CLICK AWAY

www.scilinks.org
Keyword: Energy
Code: GS5D080

Read

Read about Renato Angulo Chu, a high school student who has come up with a new use for his bicycle.

"Electricity Bike"

notes:

Bicycles are a great way to get around. They're fun to ride, especially down hills. And, as you whiz along the road, you might also think of ways in which you could improve your bike—make it safer, more <u>efficient</u>, more comfortable, or more <u>versatile</u>. In fact, the two-wheeled machines make for some cool science projects...

Electricity bike

Renato Angulo Chu had even <u>grander</u> <u>ambitions</u>. The 12th-grader from Lima, Peru, wanted to <u>address</u> some of his country's <u>economic</u> troubles.

"I see a problem in my country," Renato said. "If you go to the forests in Peru, in some places you cannot find electricity. If you go with my bicycle, you can turn on the lights."

Renato Angulo Chu adjusts his Multibike.

> What problem does Renato see in his country? <u>Underline</u> your answer.

efficient: using less energy to do the same amount of work
versatile: able to do different kinds of things

grander: bigger
ambitions: dreams
address: help solve
economic: having to do with money

Renato, 16, spent 3 years designing his special Multibike. The <u>contraption</u> looks like a <u>stationary</u> exercise bike. It has wires <u>strung</u> along the frame and a blender strapped to the back. Turning the pedals <u>operates</u> the blender....

The Multibike can work either as a stationary bike or as a bicycle able to travel city streets and country roads. It's made from inexpensive materials, and the user gets exercise while pedaling to operate a machine.

"You pedal the bike, and you can mix any drink you want," Renato said. More importantly, he added, the same <u>concept</u> could be used to bring light to houses in <u>remote</u> <u>regions</u> of the rainforest.

From: "Tinkering with the Basic Bike."
Science News for Kids, Aug 27, 2003.

notes:

> What machine does Renato's Multibike provide energy for? <u>Underline</u> your answer.

> What would Renato like his Multibike idea to provide energy for? (Circle) your answer.

contraption: machine
stationary: not moving
strung: attached
operates: runs

concept: idea
remote: far away from cities
regions: places

Look Back

> **Use what you learned in the reading to fill in the diagram below.**

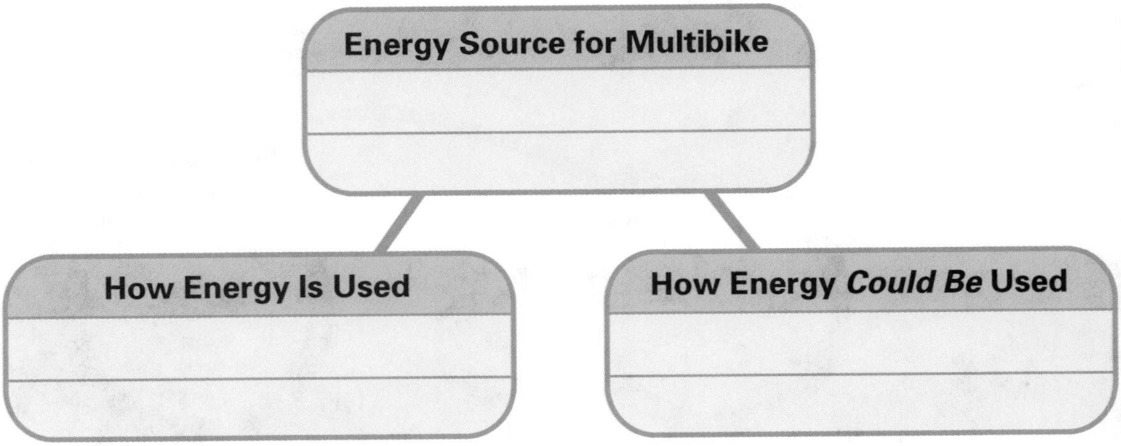

Energy Source for Multibike

How Energy Is Used

How Energy *Could Be* Used

Explore

ENERGY CHANGES

Energy comes in many different forms. Electricity is just one of them. Other forms of energy include light energy and heat energy. When you hear a noise, you are experiencing sound energy. Any object that is moving has energy of motion. Another form of energy is chemical energy, which can be stored in the chemicals found in food.

> **What forms of energy are discussed in the reading?**

_____

_____

Energy can change from any one of these forms to another. For example, a car's engine changes the chemical energy in gasoline into the energy of motion. When you drop a book, its energy of motion changes to sound energy as the book hits the floor with a loud thud.

> **Describe two other examples of energy changing from one form to another.**

_____

_____

_____

Explore

Look at the following diagram. It shows the different parts of Renato's Multibike. Notice the generator on the frame next to the back wheel. A **generator** is a device that changes the energy of motion into electricity.

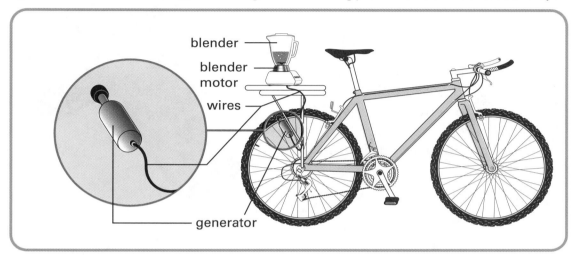

blender

blender motor

wires

generator

The generator has a small knob that presses against the wheel of the bike. As the wheel turns, the knob turns. The generator converts the **energy of motion** of magnets attached to the moving knob into electrical energy. The **electrical energy** travels along the wires to the blender. A motor on the blender uses the electrical energy to turn the blades of the blender.

> **As you learned, energy can change from one form to another. Label the point on the Multibike where energy of motion is changed to electrical energy.**

> **The electrical energy produced by the Multibike is used to power a blender. What does a blender use electrical energy to do? What type of energy does the blender change the electrical energy into?**

_____

_____

_____

> **Label the point on the Multibike where electrical energy is changed into another form of energy.**

Activity

CRANKING OUT POWER

Can you generate electricity?

What You Need:
- hand-crank generator
- light bulb with stand

Renato Angulo Chu wanted to use his Multibike to bring light to remote villages. You can see for yourself that energy of motion can be used to light a bulb.

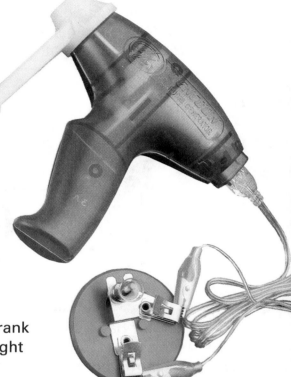

What to Do:

1. Attach the clips on the hand-crank generator to the clips on the light bulb stand.
2. Turn the crank slowly. What happens?
3. Now, turn the crank more quickly. What happens?

What Do You See?

> **What happens when you turn the crank of the generator slowly?**

_____

_____

> **What happens when you turn the crank of the generator more quickly?**

_____

_____

> **How is the hand-crank generator like the Multibike?**

_____

_____

Chapter 16

Magic Machine?

Can a machine run itself?

You are standing at the top of your sloped driveway. You're wearing a pair of in-line skates. You slowly inch forward and suddenly you are zooming downhill. Look out below!

What makes you start moving so fast? The answer is energy. **Energy** is the ability to cause motion or change. Your position when you are at the top of the driveway gives you stored energy. You stored that energy as you walked up the driveway. As you inch down the slope, the force of Earth's gravity sets you in motion. Your stored energy is changed into the energy of motion.

The conversion of stored energy into energy of motion powers more than just skaters on slopes. It can also be used to run machines. In this chapter, you'll read about a man who designed a very unusual machine that he could never get to work.

Before You Read

> **Where does the energy needed to run each of the following machines come from?**

Television _____

Pencil sharpener _____

Lawnmower _____

Flashlight _____

> **What do you do when the energy source of a flashlight runs out?**

_____

_____

SCIENCESAURUS
A STUDENT HANDBOOK
BLUE BOOK

Friction .... p. 274
Forms of
Energy .... p. 285
Energy
Changes ..... p. 286

SCILINKS®
THE WORLD'S A CLICK AWAY

www.scilinks.org
Keyword: Energy
Transfer
Code: GS5D085

Read

Read about a man who invented a machine he hoped would run itself forever.

"Something for Nothing?"

notes:

> What did people use to power the machinery that grinds grain?

> What causes the waterwheel to turn?

One of the earliest and simplest machines was the waterwheel—a wooden paddlewheel that dips into a fast-running river, so that water flowing downstream makes the wheel go round. For <u>centuries</u> people have attached waterwheels to machinery that can grind grain into flour, or lift water from a well....

Before scientists had figured out the rules about energy, it may have seemed that a waterwheel produced something for nothing. The wheel turns, <u>operating</u> some machine, but the river keeps on running. Go downstream a few hundred yards and it might be flowing just as fast as it was above the wheel.

So it's not surprising that people thought waterwheels could be turned into <u>perpetual motion machines</u> .

This waterwheel is attached to a machine that pumps water to the top of a hill.

centuries: hundreds of years
operating: running

perpetual motion machi
machines that run forever
without any outside ene

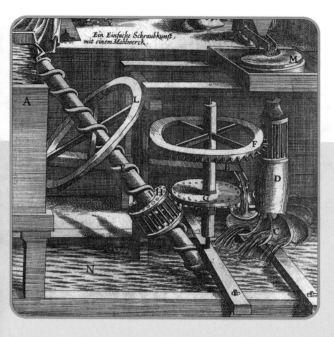

Around 1618 an Englishman named Robert Fludd came up with an idea for a waterwheel that would run without stopping. It seemed perfectly simple. Fludd arranged for water to flow out of an upper tank, <u>drive</u> a wheel around, and collect in a lower tank. Then he attached a pump (in the form of a big screw) to the waterwheel, to push water from the lower tank back to the upper one again. This arrangement, he thought, would run itself forever. What's more, it could also drive a mill to grind grain. But somehow, Fludd could never quite manage to make his perpetual motion engine work. Still, he couldn't see why it *shouldn't* work, so he and other inventors kept on trying. Not realizing they were up against a <u>fundamental</u> problem, they thought their machines would work if only they could get the designs *just right*....

From: "Something for Nothing?" *Muse* magazine, May/June 2003.

notes:

> <u>Underline</u> the sentences that describe how Robert Fludd's machine was set up.

drive: move
fundamental: very important

Look Back

> Arrange the following three phrases to describe how water cycles through Robert Fludd's waterwheel machine. Look at the picture of Robert Fludd's machine on the previous page to help you. One has been done for you.

Screw turning and pushing water up
Water sitting in raised tank
Wheel turning due to flowing water

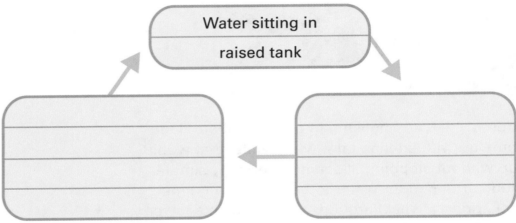

> How is the water in Fludd's machine like a flowing river that turns a waterwheel?

_____

_____

_____

> Why did Fludd think that his machine should be able to run without stopping?

_____

_____

_____

_____

> Could his machine *really* run without stopping?

_____

Explore

Moving objects have **energy of motion**. Objects that are up high have **stored energy**. The two forms of energy can change back and forth, forming a sort of cycle. For example, when you let go of a ball, it falls and its stored energy is changed into energy of motion. When it bounces back up, some of its energy of motion is changed back into stored energy. Then it falls again, and so on.

Think about the energy in Robert Fludd's machine.

> **What type of energy does the flowing water have?**

> **What type of energy does the water sitting in the upper tank of Fludd's machine have?**

> **How do these two kinds of energy change back and forth in Fludd's machine?**

 Explore

IT'S FRICTION'S FAULT

Here is how Robert Fludd imagined that his machine would work.

Fludd could never get his machine to work.

In an imaginary perpetual motion machine, energy flows in a cycle that never ends. To be a perpetual motion machine, Robert Fludd's machine would have had to produce all the energy it used. That means that all of the energy of motion produced by the machine would have to be "recycled" back into the machine to keep the machine running. No energy could escape from the cycle, or the machine would eventually stop running.

Unfortunately, perpetual motion machines *never* work—even when the designs are "just right." That's because some energy is always escaping from a machine as it runs. Most energy escaping from machines leaves because of friction. **Friction** is a force that makes it hard for two surfaces to slide past one another. When moving parts slide past each other, the friction produces heat energy. The heat energy does not help keep the machine moving. Instead, it is lost to the air around the machine.

> **Look at the perpetual motion machine above. Circle the places where you think there would be a loss of energy because of friction.**

> **Why couldn't Robert Fludd's machine run itself forever?**

How can you keep your lunch cool without a refrigerator?

Imagine that you are hiking on a hot day. You have your lunch with you—a turkey and lettuce sandwich and a carton of milk. When you sit down for a quick lunch break, you find that your milk is warm and your lettuce is wilted. Yuck!

How could you keep your lunch cool? Remember, you're on a hike, so there's no ice and no electricity to run a refrigerator. Any ideas?

In this chapter, you'll read about a teacher in Africa who solved a similar problem. He found a way to make a cooler out of local desert materials.

Before You Read

Keeping food and drink cool while hiking may be tricky. It's much easier at home.

> **How do we keep our food and drink cool at home?**

_____

_____

> **How do we keep our food and drink cool when we go places, like on a picnic?**

_____

_____

> **How do we keep our bodies cool at home and in the car?**

_____

_____

_____

Heat
Energy .... p. 289
Transfer of Heat
Energy .... p. 292

www.scilinks.org
Keyword: Heat
Transfer
Code: GS5D090

Read

Read about a man in Africa who invented a "desert refrigerator."

"Cool Pots"

notes:

In <u>hot climates</u>, fruits and vegetables begin to rot in a few days. Refrigeration gives you a headstart in the race against <u>spoilage</u>, but what if you don't have electricity, much less a fridge? A <u>Nigerian</u> teacher, Mohammed Bah Abba, won an award for a simple invention designed to keep food cool without electricity or expensive parts.

> <u>Underline</u> the two problems identified in the paragraph on this page.

hot climates: areas of the world where the weather is usually warm

spoilage: spoiling, or rotting
Nigerian: from the African country of Nigeria

Here's how it works: you put fruit, veggies, or other <u>perishable</u> food into a clay pot that's nestled inside another pot. On top of the food, you lay a damp cloth, and between the two pots, there's a layer of wet sand. As hot air dries the outer pot, it draws water from the sand. Water continuously <u>evaporates</u> from the nestled pots, carrying away heat energy and thereby cooling the inside. The <u>principle</u> is similar to the way the evaporation of sweat cools the body. As long as you keep the sand and cloth damp, the evaporation and cooling continue.

The simplicity of this invention makes it <u>practical</u> for poor people in hot climates. Inside the clay pot cooler, fruits and veggies last several weeks, instead of a few days. According to inventor Abba, the cooler is already having an <u>impact</u> on people's lives. Since it was introduced in villages in <u>semi-arid</u> northern Nigeria, more girls have enrolled in school. What's the connection? Produce from family farm plots lasts much longer than before. That means that families don't need to send girls out every day to sell produce, but can send them to school instead. And that's really cool!

From: "A Cooler for the Sahara" *A Moment of Science*,
Radio Station WFIU and Indiana University.

notes:

> How do you make sure that the coolers continue to stay cool on the inside?

> How long does food last inside the cooler compared to outside the cooler?

perishable: able to rot
evaporates: turns from liquid to gas
principle: idea

practical: well-designed
impact: effect
semi-arid: almost desert

Look Back

> Look at the diagram below. It shows what Mohammed Bah Abba's clay-pot cooler looks like on the inside. Use what you learned in the reading to label the diagram with the following terms:

Large clay pot
Small clay pot
Wet sand
Damp cloth
Fruits and vegetables

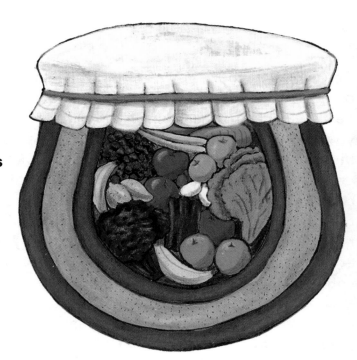

Explore

MOVEMENT OF HEAT ENERGY

When water **evaporates**—turns from liquid to gas— it absorbs heat energy from its surroundings. As the evaporated water is carried away by the air moving past the pot, the heat energy is also carried away.

> Draw arrows on the diagram above to show the movement of heat energy between the cooler and the outside air.

> Would the cooler work without water (wet sand)? Explain.

Activity

CLAY-POT COOLER

Make your own "desert refrigerator."

What You Need:

- clay pot
- smaller clay pot, same shape
- sand
- water
- dish towel
- thermometer
- lettuce leaves

What to Do:

1. Place the smaller clay pot inside the larger one.
2. Pour sand in the space between the pots until it is almost to the top.
3. Gently pour water over the sand until it is all wet.
4. Place a few lettuce leaves in the cooler. Cover the cooler with a damp dish towel.
5. Set the cooler outside in a shady spot. Place a few more lettuce leaves on the ground beside the cooler.
6. Use a thermometer to take the temperature of the air inside and outside the cooler. Record the temperatures in the chart below.
7. An hour later, remove the dish towel and take the temperature of the air inside and outside the cooler again. Record the new temperatures in the chart below.
8. Observe the lettuce leaves. Record your observations below.

What Do You See?

> **How do the leaves inside the cooler look compared to the leaves outside the cooler?**

Time of Temperature Measurement	Temperature Inside Cooler (°C)	Temperature Outside Cooler (°C)
Right away		
One Hour Later		

Explore

THE RIGHT TECHNOLOGY

Technology is any tool or product that helps people solve a problem and that was created using scientific knowledge. Refrigerators are a kind of technology we use to keep our food cold. Refrigerators work well for us because most homes in the United States have electricity.

> **What problem were the people of Nigeria facing?**

> **What technology did Mohammed Bah Abba use to solve the problem?**

> **How was the technology he used a good choice for the area where it was used?**

Explore

COMPARING TECHNOLOGIES

Have you ever used a plastic cooler filled with ice to keep your food cool on a picnic? Without the ice, the cooler probably wouldn't be as useful. How is a plastic cooler different than the clay pot cooler described in the reading?

> **Design an experiment that tests how well each cooler works. Describe your experiment below.**

Light Tricks

Chapter 18

When is seeing *not* believing?

If you've ever been to a magic show, you may know that light and mirrors can be used to play tricks on the audience. Both the "saw-the-lady-in-half" and "floating head" tricks are created by fooling your eye into believing it sees something that isn't really there.

Light can play tricks in nature, too. In this chapter, you will learn about two of these tricks.

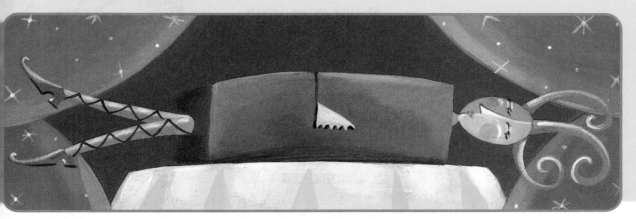

Before You Read

Some objects are dull. Others are shiny.

> **Can you name three different kinds of objects that are shiny?**

> **Based on your observations, what do you think makes something "shiny"?**

Light .... p. 309

BLUE BOOK

www.scilinks.org
Keyword:
Reflection and
Refraction
Code: GS5D095

Read

Karana is a Native American girl living alone on an island. Her only companion is Rontu, a wild dog. Karana lives on dried meat from shellfish called abalones.

"Catching the Sun"

notes:

> What do you think scared the gulls away?

I gathered two more <u>canoeloads</u> of <u>abalones</u> soon after that, mostly the sweet red ones, which I cleaned and carried to the house. Along the south part of the fence where the sun shone most of the day, I built long shelves out of branches and put the meat up to dry. Abalones are larger than your hand and twice as thick when fresh, but they shrink small in the sun so you have to dry many.

In the old days on the island there were children to keep away the gulls, which would rather feast on abalones than anything else. In one morning, if the meat was left unguarded, they could fly off with a month's <u>harvest</u>.

At first, whenever I went to the spring or to the beach, I left Rontu behind to chase them off, but he did not like this and howled all the time I was gone. Finally I tied strings to some of the abalone shells and hung them from poles. The insides of the shells are bright and catch the sun and they turn one way and another in the wind. After that I had little trouble with the gulls.

From: *Island of the Blue Dolphins*, by Scott O'Dell.

canoeloads: canoes full
abalones: a type of shellfish
harvest: catch

Look Back

> **What problem did Karana face?**

> **How did she use light to solve her problem?**

Explore

REFLECTED LIGHT

Most of the light around us comes from the sun. We can also make light using electricity and light bulbs.

Light travels in straight lines until it hits something. Some of the light is absorbed by the object it hits, and some is **reflected**, or bounced back. You can see an object because some of the light it reflects travels to your eyes. In the diagram at right, you can see how light from a light bulb travels in a straight line until it is reflected by an object. The viewer can see the light reflected by the object.

Certain objects reflect more light than others. The material on the inside of abalone shells reflects light so well that it looks like the light is actually coming from the shell itself.

> **In the diagram at right, draw the path that sunlight takes when it is reflected off the abalone shells and into the bird's eyes.**

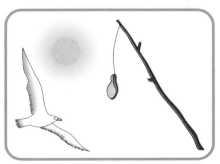

Read

Mafatu is a boy stranded on a desert island. One day, Mafatu accidentally drops his only knife into the water. He stares down at the water, trying to decide what to do.

"So Very Near, and Yet…"

notes:

> Why was Mafatu scared to get his knife?

> What made it hard for Mafatu to tell how far away his knife was?

With dismay the boy watched it <u>descend</u>. It spiraled rapidly, catching the sunlight as it dropped down, down to the sandy bottom. And there it lay, just under the edge of a <u>branching staghorn</u>. Mafatu eyed it uncertainly. His knife—the knife he had labored so hard to shape…. He knew what he ought to do: he should dive and retrieve it. To make another knife so fine would take days. Without it he was seriously handicapped. He *must* get his knife! But…

The reef-wall looked dark and forbidding in the fading light. Its black holes were the home of the giant *feké*—the octopus…. The boy drew back in sudden panic. He had never dived as deep as this. It might be even deeper than he thought, for the clarity of the water <u>confused all scale of distance</u>. The knife looked so very near, and yet…There it lay, gleaming palely.

From: *Call It Courage*, by Armstrong Sperry.

descend: sink
branching staghorn: part of a coral reef

confused all scale of distance: made it hard to tell how far away an object was

Look Back

> **How far away did the knife *look* to Mafatu?**

> **How far away did Mafatu think the knife might *actually* be?**

> **Mafatu explains that the water made it hard to tell how far away the knife really was. Based on your answers above, do you think the water made the knife look closer than it really was or farther away than it really was?**

Activity

LIGHT TRICK

What You Need:
- shallow bowl (not see-through)
- penny
- water

1. Place a penny at the bottom of a shallow bowl.
2. Stand a few feet away from the bowl. The penny should be just hidden from view by the sides of the bowl.
3. Now fill the bowl with water. Stand in the same place you did before.

> **Can you see the penny now?**

Explore

REFRACTED LIGHT

Look at a diagram below. It shows how light rays reflect off of an underwater object and travel to a viewer's eye.

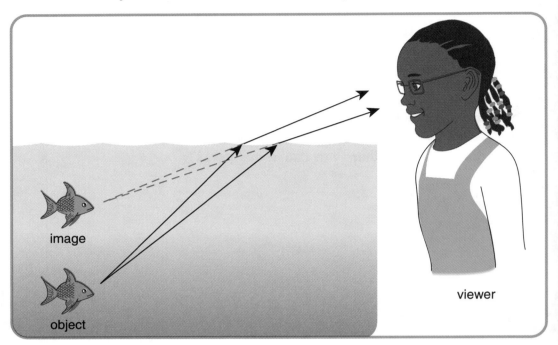

image

object

viewer

Light rays reflecting off the object are **refracted** as they leave the water. That means that they change direction slightly. When the rays enter your eye, your brain "thinks" they have traveled in a straight line from the object to your eye. Why? Because light rays always travel in straight lines. So the brain forms an **image** of where the object would be if the reflected light rays had traveled in a straight line without refracting. But that image isn't where the object actually is!

> **Was Mafatu right? Is his knife deeper than it looks? Explain.**

UNIT 3: Physical Science

What Did We Learn?

How does the poison dart frog make its toxic chemicals?

How can a spy uncover a message written in invisible ink?

How is energy converted in the "Multibike"?

Why can't perpetual motion machines ever really work?

How does evaporating water allow a desert refrigerator to cool food?

How can refraction change the way you see an object underwater?

UNIT 4: Natural Resources and the Environment

DID YOU KNOW?

In some areas of the United States you can find deformed frogs that have more than four legs.

Chapter 19
On the Dung Trail
Find out: How can you build a fire if you can't find any wood?

Chapter 20
Early Warning System
Find out: What can an animal's deformed leg tell you about its environment?

Chapter 21
Paging Dr. Nature
Find out: Can tree bark save your life?

Could mammoth poop keep you warm?

If you have ever gone on a long camping trip, you know that you have to carry a lot of things to keep you safe. You need a tent to protect you from the rain, a sleeping bag to keep you warm, and lots of food and water so that you do not get hungry or thirsty. Some camping areas do not allow you to collect firewood. So, if you want to cook your food, you will also need to bring along some firewood or some other source of fuel.

Tens of thousands of years ago, humans living on the continents of Africa and Asia began a long journey to North America. (Today an ocean separates Asia from North America. But 50,000 years ago, there was no ocean between the northern parts of the two continents.) The trip was a long one, and people would have needed a source of fuel for keeping warm and cooking food. Since there were almost no trees in this cold landscape, scientists have wondered what the people might have used for fuel. In this chapter, you'll read about a scientist who came up with one explanation that may surprise you.

Before You Read

Have you ever been camping? If not, maybe you've seen people camping in a movie.

> **Why do people need to burn fuel when they are camping?**

_____

_____

SCIENCESAURUS
A STUDENT HANDBOOK
BLUE BOOK

Getting and Using Energy .... p. 77
Energy from Plants and Animals .... p. 328

> **People often make a fire using firewood. Can you think of any other sources of fuel people use when they are camping?**

_____

_____

THE WORLD'S A CLICK AWAY

www.scilinks.org
Keyword: Natural Resources
Code: GS5D100

Read

Read about a scientist who thinks he might know how people stayed warm during their long journey from Asia to North America.

"A Different Kind of Fuel"

notes:

If you think traveling to Alaska in the winter sounds cold today, imagine what it was like thousands of years ago.

Before the invention of central heating and hot cocoa, it would have been too cold for people to <u>migrate</u> to North America through the <u>frigid tundra</u>—without trees or firewood. Or so scientists thought.

Now, researchers suggest that our <u>ancestors</u> could have survived cold-weather travel if they had taken advantage of all the <u>dung</u> lying around.

More than 50,000 years ago, Alaska was connected to northern Russia by a land bridge that is now largely underwater. Yet [evidence shows that] people didn't make the crossing until about 14,000 years ago.... Scientists have long blamed the delay on cold weather and a lack of fuel for heating and cooking.

> (Circle) the kind of fuel scientists first thought people migrating to North America would have needed for heating and cooking.

migrate: move
frigid: very cold

tundra: regions where it is very cold and there are almost no trees

ancestors: people who came before us
dung: animal poop

The yellow areas used to be land 50,000 years ago. Today, these areas are underwater except for a few small islands.

That might not be the best explanation, says [scientist] David Rhode..., who has studied the dung-burning habits of modern Tibetans . To heat their tents and cook their food, Rhode has observed, a single family...burns between 25 and 40 kilograms of dried yak dung in the summer and twice that in the winter. That's a lot of dung....

Thousands of years ago, Rhode says, the route from Russia to Alaska would have been bursting with big plant-eating animals, like bison, mammoths, horses, and wooly rhinoceroses. With animals comes waste . There should have been plenty of dried dung to fuel the trip.

So, why the delay? Maybe our ancestors took a while to realize the value of the poop along their path!

From: "A Human Migration Fueled by Dung?" *Science News for Kids*, Aug 13, 2003.

notes:

> What activities do modern Tibetans burn dung for? Underline your answer.

> Circle the kind of fuel David Rhode thinks would have been available to people migrating to North America.

> What did big animals on the route eat?

Tibetans: people from the Asian country of Tibet

yak: a large plant-eating animal kept by people for milk, meat, and work

waste: poop

129

Look Back

Use what you learned in the reading to answer the following questions

> **What explanation did scientists used to give for the fact that people waited thousands of years to migrate from Russia to North America?**

_____

_____

> **Why does scientist David Rhode think that this explanation is not correct?**

_____

_____

> **What evidence did David Rhode base his conclusion on?**

_____

_____

_____

_____

_____

Explore

ENERGY FROM DUNG

You probably never thought of animal dung—or poop—as a source of fuel. But people have been using it ever since they started raising plan eating animals, such as sheep, goats, and cows. Like firewood, dung is a source of fuel because it contains energy.

> **Look back at the reading. What kinds of animals lived along the route from Russia Alaska?**

_____

_____

_____

(continued on next pag

(continued from previous page)

Why does dung contain energy? Plants are made up of materials that contain energy. When an animal eats plants, it gets energy from the plant material that it digests. But it doesn't digest all parts of the plant. Some of the plant material passes out of the animal without being digested. That means that the dung of plant-eating animals contains energy still stored in the undigested plant material.

Plants use energy from sunlight to grow and make all of their plant parts. Animals that eat plants get their energy from the plant parts that they eat.

This preserved mammoth dung contains lots of undigested plant material.

Some people use dung as a source of fuel.

> **Fill in the diagram below with the terms provided to show the path that energy takes from the sun all the way to a person's cooking stove.**

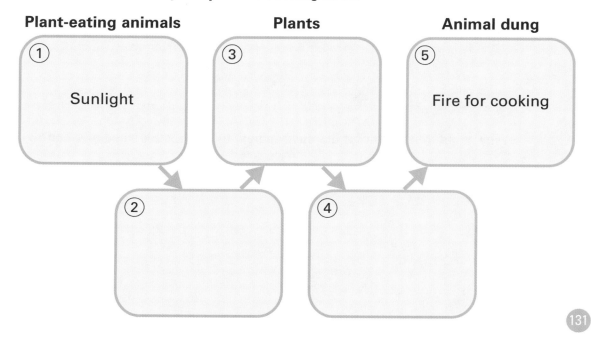

Plant-eating animals   Plants   Animal dung

① Sunlight

③

⑤ Fire for cooking

②

④

Explore

A Good Choice

There is often more than one source of fuel available for use in an area. People will often use the type of fuel that is the cheapest or most readily available. Dung has been used as a source of fuel for thousands of years. It may not sound very clean, but it is not any messier than other kinds of fuel. In fact, when it is dried, dung does not smell and it looks very much like dried dirt. Many people around the world still use dried dung as a fuel source today. Look at the two pictures below.

> Draw a circle around the person you think would use dung to build a fire.

> Why would dung be a good choice for this person?

_____

_____

_____

_____

> Why might it be better for the environment to use dung instead of wood?

_____

_____

_____

_____

_____

What can a deformed frog tell you about its environment?

What would you think if one day, while swimming in a lake, you found a frog with three legs instead of four? You'd probably think, "That poor frog lost a leg." But what if you found a frog that had five legs? You might be a little concerned! Having five legs instead of four is a deformity. An animal can be born with a **deformity** that it inherited from its parents. Or, a deformity at birth may be caused by something in the animal's environment.

In this chapter, you'll read about an animal whose deformities might tell scientists a lot about the environment.

Before You Read

> **If you wanted to find out whether an environment was polluted or not, what signs would you look for? Name at least three signs that tell you that an environment is polluted.**

_____

_____

_____

_____

_____

_____

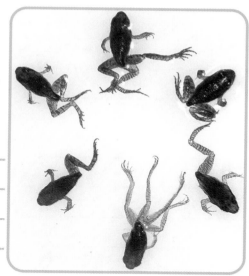

SCIENCESAURUS
A STUDENT HANDBOOK
BLUE BOOK

SCI LINKS.
THE WORLD'S A CLICK AWAY

www.scilinks.org
Keyword: Pollution
Code: GS5D105

Read

Read about how deformities in frogs help warn scientists that an environment could be polluted.

"Sounding an Alarm"

notes:

Frogs survived the catastrophic extinction of the dinosaurs. But strangely, the world's frogs and toads have suddenly begun to disappear. Some species that were common 20 years ago are now rare or extinct. And individual frogs are showing up with deformities such as too many legs.... Scientists are not exactly sure what is going on.

Pollution may have caused this northern leopard frog to grow a fifth leg.

>What two problems have scientists found with frogs? Underline your answer.

But scientists do agree that because frogs drink and breathe through their thin skin they are especially vulnerable to pesticides and pollution. A deformed frog often indicates that all is not well with the environment. And frogs live just about everywhere on Earth.

catastrophic: big and sudden
extinction: dying out
species: kinds

deformities: body parts that are not "normal"
vulnerable to: easily affected by

pesticides: chemicals use to kill insects and other small animals
indicates: points out

Frogs are <u>amphibians</u>, which means "double life." They generally hatch in water as tadpoles and end up living on land as fully formed frogs. Frogs' skin must stay moist, so they're usually found in wet places.

Because frogs are so sensitive to environmental changes, they act as an early warning system. Their <u>dwindling</u> numbers may be a sign that our planet is not as clean and healthy as it once was. By studying how frogs are affected by the environment around them, scientists may be able to predict—and sound an alarm—that a neighborhood needs to cut back on lawn <u>fertilizers</u> or that a chemical-dumping factory should clean up its act. The hidden message in frogs' familiar peeps and croaks? "I'm jumpy for a reason!"

From: "Weird World of Frogs,"
National Geographic World, March 2002.

notes:

> How do frogs act as an "early warning system"?

> How can you tell that the last sentence is a joke and not a scientific fact?

amphibians: animals that start life in water but live on land as adults

dwindling: decreasing
fertilizers: chemicals used to help grass grow

Look Back

Scientists who want to know how an environment is changing will often study an indicator species in that environment. An **indicator species** is a kind of plant or animal that reacts quickly to changes in the environment. By looking for changes to the indicator species, scientists can find out how the environment as a whole might be changing.

> **What indicator species were described in the reading?**

_____

> **What changes did scientists notice in the indicator species?**

_____

_____

_____

> **What did the changes in the indicator species tell scientists about the environment as a whole?**

_____

_____

_____

> **According to the reading, what might have caused the changes to the environment? Name at least three things.**

_____

_____

_____

_____

_____

Explore

FROGS AS INDICATOR SPECIES

Polluting chemicals from lawns and
factories usually end up in rivers,
streams, and lakes. Sometimes the
water in these rivers, streams, and lakes
looks clear and tastes fine but still
contains pollution.

> **Why are frogs more easily affected by polluting chemicals than some other animals?**

> **Why do you think frogs are useful as indicator species?**

> **Why do you think it's important that scientists look at indicator species to see if an environment is polluted? Why don't they just rely on the water's taste or appearance?**

Science Journal

Imagine that there is a large fertilizer company located in your town. The company just opened up a new factory near a river. Lately, frogs with deformities have been found in the river.

Some people believe that the deformities must be due to chemicals that are washed from the factory grounds to the river by rainwater. Others believe that the deformities are due to parasites, tiny organisms that live on the frogs' bodies and make them sick. Still others believe that the deformities are caused by harmful radiation from the sun.

> **In the space below, write a letter to the president of the fertilizer company. In your letter, explain what evidence you have that the environment is changing. Use what you have learned about indicator species to support your argument. Finally, explain why it's important that the company stop making fertilizers at the new factory until scientists can figure out what is going on.**

Don't feel good, have a fever? Try some wood, says the beaver.

It's Monday morning and your alarm is going off. HONK HONK HONK. Time for school! But you don't feel much like getting out of bed. You feel hot and your throat hurts. Uh oh, it looks like you're sick.

Where do you go when you get really sick? You probably go to the doctor or to a hospital. But long before there were doctors and hospitals, people had to find other ways to cure their sicknesses. Often, they found those cures in nature.

In this chapter, you'll read about different kinds of "natural" medicine used today and long ago.

Before You Read

If you get very sick, you can get medicine from a doctor. But before you get very sick, you might try a natural cure to help you feel better. Some plants and foods are thought to heal people and keep them from getting very sick.

> **Name at least three plants or foods that are some-times used to help people get over an illness.**

_____

_____

_____

SCIENCESAURUS
A STUDENT HANDBOOK
BLUE BOOK

Material Resources   p. 329
Many Different People Contribute to Science   p. 367

SC*L*INKS.
THE WORLD'S A CLICK AWAY

www.scilinks.org
Keyword: Medicine from Plants
Code: GS5D110

> **Think of a time when you felt sick but did not take any medicine or go to the doctor. What did you do or take to make yourself feel better?**

_____

_____

Read

Read about an imaginary pill that contains some strange ingredients.

Silly Pilly

notes:

If you feel sick,
If you feel ill,
Try swallowing
This ten-pound pill.
It's <u>fortified</u> with lizard knee,
The eye of <u>newt</u>,
<u>Extract of</u> bee.
It satisfies your daily need
For <u>rhubarb</u> root
And maple seed.
With wild weeds and five raw eggs,
It helps you grow
Grass on your legs.
It clears your head,
It clears your skin,
And if you're fat,
It makes you thin.
So open wide and bottoms up!
Just gulp it down—
And don't throw up.

> (Circle) all the Silly Pilly
  ingredients that come from
  plants or animals.

> <u>Underline</u> all the ways that
  the poem claims Silly Pilly
  helps you.

From: *Laugh-Eteria,* by Douglas Florian.

fortified: made stronger
newt: a kind of salamander,
  an amphibian

extract of: part of
rhubarb: a kind of vegetab
  plant

Look Back

The Silly Pilly doesn't really exist—except in the author's imagination. But it is true that many medicines are made using plant and animal materials.

> In the left-hand column, list all the Silly Pilly ingredients that come from plants. In the right-hand column, list all the ingredients that come from animals.

Ingredients from Plants	Ingredients from Animals

> Not all plant and animal parts help heal people, and not all pills do what their labels say they will. Why do you think that this pill won't do what the poem claims it will?

_____

_____

_____

Project

HERBAL SUPPLEMENTS

Look at the bottle of herbal supplement your teacher has given you. An **herbal supplement** is a product made from a type of leafy plant called an herb. Many people take herbal supplements to improve their health, although not everyone believes they really work.

Study the label on the bottle. Then answer the following questions.

> **What plant do these pills contain?**

_____

> **How is the plant supposed to improve health?**

_____

⌐Read

The Silly Pilly is not real. But here's a plant medicine that is. Read a story about a Spanish soldier who was saved by the bark of a tree.

"Bitter Water"

notes:

> <u>Underline</u> the sentence that tells you that this story might not be true.

> Why did the water taste bitter?

Quinine isn't something most Americans keep in their medicine cabinets. But quinine has had a major <u>influence</u> on the world of medicine.

Quinine is the drug used to treat patients with <u>malaria</u>, a disease spread by certain kinds of mosquitoes. Legend says quinine was discovered by accident in the early 1600s.

A Spanish soldier in Peru had an extremely high fever and chills caused by malaria. His <u>comrades</u> left him behind to die. The high fever made him so thirsty that he crawled to a nearby shallow pond to drink. Although the pond water tasted bitter, he drank it anyway, then fell asleep.

When he awoke, his fever had gone down. He rejoined his military company and told them of the <u>miraculous</u> pond water. They examined the water and discovered that its bitter taste came from the bark of a log lying in the pool. The soldier had accidentally discovered that the bark of the cinchona tree could cure malaria.

For almost two hundred years, the bark of the cinchona tree was made into a powder and used to cure malaria. Today <u>synthetic</u> drugs are more often used to treat the disease.

From: *Accidents May Happen: Fifty Inventions Discovered by Mistake,* by Charlotte Foltz Jones.

influence: effect
malaria: a disease that gives people a high fever
comrades: friends

miraculous: amazing
synthetic: made by people in the laboratory

Look Back

> **Use what you learned in the reading to fill in the concept map below.**

Soldier's Disease	→	Cure for Disease	→	Source of Cure

Explore

WHAT ABOUT THE TREE?

Cinchona trees grow in the rainforests of South America. Look at the picture at right. It shows a person taking the bark off a cinchona tree.

> **How do you think taking the bark off the tree might affect the tree?**

Once people found out about how cinchona bark cured malaria, they started stripping it off of all the cinchona trees. Without their bark, the trees died. A few hundred years later, it was hard to find a cinchona tree growing wild in Peru. Later, people started planting the trees again and taking care to protect them.

Science Journal

Biodiversity is the term scientists use to refer to the variety of plants and animals in a given place. Some places, like the Amazonian rainforest in South America, have many different kinds of plants and animals. Biodiversity in the rainforest is very high.

Many natural medicines, including quinine, have been discovered in the rainforest. For thousands of years, people in the rainforest have eaten plant leaves and roots as food. Often, they discovered that one of these plants helped a sick person get better.

Imagine that a logging company wants to clear large areas of a rainforest in order to use the wood from the rainforest trees and provide grazing land for local cattle farmers.

> **Write a letter to the logging company explaining why you think it is important to protect biodiversity in the rainforest. Use examples from the chapter to help you.**

Many medicines come from natural sources.

UNIT 4: Natural Resources and the Environment

What Did We Learn?

CHAPTER 19

What makes dung a good choice as a source of fuel?

_____

_____

_____

_____

CHAPTER 20

Why do frogs make good "indicator species"?

_____

_____

_____

_____

_____

_____

CHAPTER 21

Why is biodiversity important?

_____

_____

_____

_____

_____

_____

UNIT 5: Science, Technology, and Society

DID YOU KNOW?
The idea for the recipe for moder[n] paper came from the way that was[ps] make paper nest[s] by chewing woo[d]

Chapter 22
The Invention of Paper
Find out: What can wasps teach us about making paper?

Chapter 23 **A New Beak**
Find out: Why don't bald eagles mind going to the dentist?

Chapter 24
Animated Movies
Find out: How many people did it take to create *The Hulk*?

The Invention of Paper

Sometimes inventors steal ideas from nature.

Each person in the United States uses an average of 580 pounds of paper every year. That's over a pound and a half per day!

Do you know where paper comes from? The paper we use today is made from wood that comes from trees. But thousands of years ago, people didn't have paper. Instead, they used to write on thin strips of bamboo, sheets of silk, or even the dried skin of animals.

In this chapter, you'll read about a person who used an idea from nature to invent the paper we use today.

Before You Read

We all use a lot of paper every day. When you think of paper, you probably think of notebook paper. But not all paper is made for writing on. For example, napkins are a kind of paper that is used to wipe your mouth and hands after eating.

> **List five different paper products you use every day.**

SCIENCE SAURUS
A STUDENT HANDBOOK
BLUE BOOK

Material
Resources ... p. 328

> **What is one way you could use less paper?**

SCI LINKS.
THE WORLD'S A CLICK AWAY

www.scilinks.org
Keyword: Paper
Code: GS5D115

Read

Read about early kinds of paper, and how modern paper was invented.

"Paper Home"

notes:

> (Circle) all the ingredients Ts'ai Lun used to make paper.

Why do you think that paper allowed the Chinese to become "the most advanced culture in the world"? Jot down any ideas you have.

Make a list of the most <u>influential</u> people in the world's history. You might include Julius Caesar, Cleopatra, Confucius, Queen Victoria, Gandhi, Thomas Edison, Marie Curie, Albert Einstein, Ts'ai Lun.

Wait! Who is Ts'ai Lun?

Believe it or not, your life is influenced enormously by Ts'ai Lun!

Ts'ai Lun was a Chinese <u>court official</u> almost two thousand years ago. In 105 A.D. he invented paper as we know it today. He mashed Mulberry bark, <u>hemp</u>, <u>rags</u>, and water into a pulp, pressed out the liquid, and hung the thin mat in the sun to dry.

People had writing materials as early as 3500 B.C., but paper allowed the Chinese to become the most advanced culture in the world. Surprisingly, Ts'ai Lun's method of papermaking was not introduced in Europe for another thousand years. In 1151 the first <u>paper mill</u> was built in Spain.

Over the centuries the demand for paper grew—especially with the invention of the <u>printing press</u>. While the need for paper grew, the supply of rags shrank. Besides, paper-making was very time-consuming.

influential: causing important change
court official: person who worked for the Emperor

hemp: plant with tough fibers
rags: old bits of clothing, often made of cotton

paper mill: machine that makes paper
printing press: machine that uses ink to print words on paper

The world needed a solution.

One day in the early 1700s (no one is sure of the date), René-Antoine Ferchault de Réaumur, a French scientist, was walking in the woods. As he walked he spotted a wasp's nest and, since the wasps weren't home, stopped to investigate.

Suddenly Réaumur realized that the wasp's nest was made of paper. How did the wasps make paper without using rags? How did they make paper without using chemicals, fire, and mixing tanks? What did the wasps know that humans couldn't figure out?

It was quite simple. The wasps made paper by chewing small twigs or tiny bits of rotting logs and mixing them with saliva and stomach juices. Réaumur studied the digestive system of the wasp and presented his findings to the French Royal Academy in 1719.

It took more than 150 years before a machine was invented that could chew wood <u>efficiently</u> enough to make <u>wood pulp</u> paper <u>commercially</u>. But thanks to Réaumur and the wasps' <u>vacant</u> house, paper is widely used in today's society.

From: *Accidents May Happen: Fifty Inventions Discovered by Mistake,* by Charlotte Foltz Jones.

notes:

> <u>Underline</u> all the ingredients the wasps use to make their paper nests.

> What is most paper made out of today?

French Royal Academy: organization that encourages and supports scientific study
efficiently: well

wood pulp: wood that has been ground up and mixed with water

commercially: as a business to make money
vacant: empty

Look Back

> **What was Ts'ai Lun's paper made out of?**

> **What was the wasp's nest paper made out of?**

> **What is most paper made out of today?**

All kinds of paper have one thing in common: they are all made from plant fibers. For example, the rags used to make Ts'ai Lun's paper are often made of fibers from the cotton plant. **Plant fibers** are the tough strands of material found in all plants. Plant fibers are what make plants strong enough to support their own weight. Plant fiber is also what makes paper strong.

> **What is the source of plant fibers in each kind of paper listed above?**

Explore

AN IDEA FROM NATURE

Paper is an example of a technology. **Technology** is any tool or product that improves people's lives or helps them do a job. Paper allows people to write down their ideas and share them with others.

Engineers—people who design technology— often look to nature when coming up with new ideas for technology.

> **What idea from nature did Réaumur use when designing a new way to make paper?**

Activity

MAKE YOUR OWN RECYCLED PAPER

Today, most paper is made from wood that comes directly from trees. But cutting down too many trees to make paper can lead to many problems in the environment. In this activity, you will make recycled paper—paper made from old paper that has already been used. The wood fibers that made up the old paper are still good. They just need to be separated and made into new paper. Recycling paper in this way can help save trees.

What You Need:

- 2 sheets of newspaper
- blender or food processor
- water
- large plastic tub
- 2 tablespoons white glue
- stirring spoon
- screen
- clothes iron

What to Do:

1. Tear the paper into small pieces. Put the pieces in the blender with enough water to make the mixture watery (about 2 or 3 cups). Blend on medium to high until you can't see any bits of paper. Then blend for another 2 minutes.

2. Place the screen at the bottom of the large plastic tub.

3. Pour enough water into the tub until it is about 4 inches deep. Stir in the 2 tablespoons of glue and the paper mixture from the blender. Stir together until well mixed.

(continued on next page)

(continued from previous page)

4. Lift the screen up very slowly. It should take you 20–30 seconds to lift the screen to the top of the tub. Let the water drip into the tub for about a minute. Then place your screen somewhere where it can dry.

5. Once the paper is dry, you can gently peel it off the screen.

6. Have your teacher iron your paper flat. Trim the edges with scissors.

7. Write a letter to a friend on your piece of paper.

Think About It:

> **Compare the paper you made to the paper made by the wasps. What very important basic ingredient do they have in common?**

_____

_____

Remember that the wasps mixed the wood they chewed up with saliva and stomach juices. Saliva and stomach juices contain chemicals that break down food into smaller parts so that it can be digested.

> **How do you think saliva and stomach juices help the wasps make paper for their nests? (Hint: Compare the wasps' way of making paper with the steps you followed to make your own paper.)**

_____

_____

_____

_____

_____

_____

A New Beak

Chapter 23

What's a bird without a beak to do?

Imagine an eagle eating a fish that it pulled out of a river. The eagle does not have sharp teeth, like a wolf, that can tear up the food. What it does have is a strong, pointed beak. It uses its beak to rip the fish into bite-sized pieces it can eat. Can you imagine, then, what would happen to an eagle that lost its beak? How would it feed itself?

Technology to the rescue! Technology is any tool or product that improves the lives of people—or sometimes—animals. In this chapter, you'll read about an eagle that was saved by technology and a team of thoughtful dentists.

Before You Read

A **prosthesis** is an artificial body part used to replace a natural part that is damaged or missing. Sometimes people injured in accidents or war need to have a prosthesis made. The prosthesis cannot do everything the original body part did. But it helps the person do many of the same activities he or she did before the injury.

> **Do you have any friends or relatives who wear a prosthesis? List any prosthesis you might have seen in real life or on TV. What body part does each prosthesis replace? How does the prosthesis help the person who wears it?**

_____

_____

_____

SCIENCESAURUS
A STUDENT HANDBOOK
BLUE BOOK
Designing
Technology p. 358

SCI LINKS
THE WORLD'S A CLICK AWAY
www.scilinks.org
Keyword: Engineer
Code: GS5D120

Read

In 2002, an injured bald eagle was found in Canada. Most of its beak had been shot off by a hunter. A team of helpful dentists came to its rescue.

"Making a Beak"

notes:

> How many beaks does Dr. Andrews think the team will make before they get one that's just right?

> Why does Dr. Andrews think they have to make so many beaks before they get it right?

Canada: August 19, 2002

A bald eagle that was left for dead after its beak was shot off is alive and tearing its prey to shreds again thanks to a Canadian dentist who <u>fashioned</u> an <u>artificial</u> <u>bill</u> out of [plastic].

Now Dr. Brian Andrews is working to improve on the <u>prototype</u>, which is pinned to the tiny bit of beak left after the gunshot, so the $4\frac{1}{2}$-year-old bird of prey can one day return to the wild.

"Because this is <u>new ground</u> for us, and I'm new at this, we expect to make three or four or five or even a dozen until we get it right," Andrews said last week from his dental [office] in Nanaimo, British Columbia. ...

He based the design, complete with breathing holes, on a picture of an eagle on a recent cover of National Geographic magazine as well as [on] a dried beak <u>specimen</u>. ...

The [people who rescued the eagle] nursed the 18-pound (8-kilogram) bird back to health, but the soft, remaining <u>nub</u> of its bill prevented it from eating anything but small <u>morsels</u>.

> <u>Underline</u> what Dr. Andrews based his beak design on.

fashioned: made
artificial: made by people
bill: beak
prototype: early design model

new ground: something that has never been done before
specimen: sample
nub: base
morsels: bits of food

Fred Leak, the dental technician who made the first beak, takes care of the eagle and continues to improve its plastic beak.

Andrews [created a model of the] beak and took it to a <u>dental technician</u>, [Fred Leak,] who made a <u>replica</u> out of [the same plastic] used to make some false teeth and mouth guards for hockey players, he said.

He stained the [new beak] yellow, to make it look realistic. The bird took to it immediately.

"He's tearing at his prey. When we first put it on, he gave us this nice, great big yawn and squawk, and we were quite thrilled that it stayed together," Andrews said. ...

"I'm fond of wildlife. I'm a carver and I make duck <u>decoys</u> as a hobby. I figured: I can carve a wooden beak, maybe I can make a plastic one for this guy," he said.

From: "Canadian dentist gives eagle new beak, waives bill," *Planet Ark*, August 19, 2002.

dental technician: someone who makes devices for dentists
replica: copy

decoys: wooden animals carved to look like the real thing

notes:

> How did missing most of its beak cause problems for the eagle?

Look Back

Answer the following questions based on what you learned in the reading about the prosthesis that the injured eagle wore.

> **What body part did the prosthesis replace?**

_____

> **What material did they use to make it?**

_____

> **How was it attached to the eagle?**

_____

_____

> **What did the eagle use the prosthesis for?**

_____

Explore

USING PROTOTYPES

A **prototype** is an early model of a design. Engineers—people who design technology—usually build many different designs before they get one that works well.

Fred Leak made four prototypes of the prosthetic beak before he got the one that worked best. The eagle ripped the first beak right off. The second beak trapped water between what was left of the real beak and the prosthetic beak. This caused the real beak to soften. The third beak was too big. The fourth beak was the one that worked.

> **How did prototypes help Fred Leak get a design that worked well?**

_____

_____

_____

Explore

The diagram on the left shows the steps engineers follow when designing a new technology.

> **Study the diagram on the left. Then complete the diagram on the right to show the steps the dentists followed when they designed the prosthetic beak.**

Identify a Problem

What was the problem?

Think of a Solution

What was the solution?

Test the Solution

How did they test this solution?

Decide If the Solution Worked

Did this solution work? Yes or No?

1st solution: 3rd solution:

2nd solution: 4th solution:

If Not, Think of a New Solution

How was each new solution different from the one before?

2nd solution:

3rd solution:

4th solution:

Explore

USING SKILLS TO DESIGN TECHNOLOGY

Sometimes people lose teeth that have rotted or died. A dentist, such as Dr. Andrews, can replace these teeth with false teeth. A dental technician, such as Fred Leak, makes the false teeth out of plastic or another material. They both make sure that the new teeth are the right size and shape so that they work as well as the original teeth. Sometimes they have to keep adjusting the false teeth until they fit and work just right.

> **What skills from his profession—or work—allowed Fred Leak to help the bald eagle?**

> **What skills from his personal interests—or hobbies—allowed Dr. Andrews to help the bald eagle? (Hint: Look back at the reading.)**

This case displays several of the different prosthetic beaks that Fred Leak designed for the eagle.

He's green, he's mean, but is he real?

The Incredible Hulk is a comic book character that was first created in 1962 by writer Stan Lee. The Hulk was an ordinary man who turned into a giant, green monster when he got very angry. In 2003, the movie *The Hulk* came out. The movie had real actors, but it also had a character made using computer technology—the big, green Hulk himself.

In this chapter, you will learn how technology was used to create the Hulk. You'll also see how a team of people with different skills worked together on the project.

Before You Read

How is a picture of an object different from the object itself?

> **Draw a picture of a pencil in the space below.**

> **Compare your drawing to the pencil. What information about the pencil can you get by looking at the actual pencil but not by looking at the picture?**

SCI LINKS.
THE WORLD'S A CLICK AWAY

www.scilinks.org
Keyword:
Computer
Technology
Code: GS5D125

Read

Read about how a special team of people used technology to create the Hulk on the big screen.

"The Hulk Comes Alive!"

notes:

In the new movie *The Hulk* the monstrous green superhero stands 15 feet tall and weighs two tons. Scary! But the huge star didn't start out so impressive. He <u>evolved</u> from pencil sketches on paper and a ten-inch-tall clay model. How'd he become the monster he is today? It took artists, sculptors, animators, and a ton of cool technology.

1 <u>Laser</u> Scan A clay sculpture is created from sketches of the Hulk. Technicians place the sculpture onto a <u>turntable</u>. "As it <u>rotates</u>, we <u>scan</u> the model with a laser light," explains Paul Giacoppo, Creature Supervisor (yep, that's a real job title!). "The laser makes a 3-D picture on a computer of the mini-Hulk that can then be <u>altered</u>."

> What tool did the technicians use to scan the sculpture and make a 3-D picture of it on the computer?

evolved: was developed
laser: concentrated light beam
turntable: disk that turns around, like a merry-go-round

rotates: turns around
scan: move across
altered: changed

2 Inside The Computer The 3-D computer model is "the real starting point for what our <u>digital</u> character will look like," says Giacoppo. With clicks of a computer mouse, Giacoppo and his team add more muscles to the Hulk's body, alter his face to look meaner, and make the Hulk appear as powerful and impressive as possible.

3 <u>Animating</u> The Muscled Monster Now the computer animators take over. They're the people who draw (in the computer) everything the Hulk does in the movie. The movie director shot the movie with someone moving a stick with a picture of Hulk's face on it to <u>represent</u> the Hulk's movements. That's what the human actors reacted to. Later the stick is replaced with the animated drawings made of the Hulk playing his part as a digital character.

4 The Hulk Comes Alive! The team that includes 42 animators, 7 <u>digital artists</u>, and 10 creature developers works for about three months to finish the Hulk. When he finally jumps onto the screen, the superhero is capable of running 150 miles an hour and leaping two miles. It takes *a lot* to create a giant green <u>humanoid</u>!

From: "The Hulk Comes Alive!"
National Geographic Kids, July/August 2003.

notes:

> What do the animators do to the Hulk's image?

digital: made on the computer
animating: bringing to "life" on the computer

represent: stand for
digital artists: people who draw using computers

humanoid: human-like creature

Look Back

The reading describes a process with many steps for creating an animated character.

> **Put the following steps in order to show how the animated Hulk was created.**
> • Change the appearance of the 3-D image.
> • Create clay model of the Hulk.
> • Create pencil sketches of the Hulk.
> • Make the Hulk move around in the movie.
> • Create a 3-D image of the Hulk on the computer.

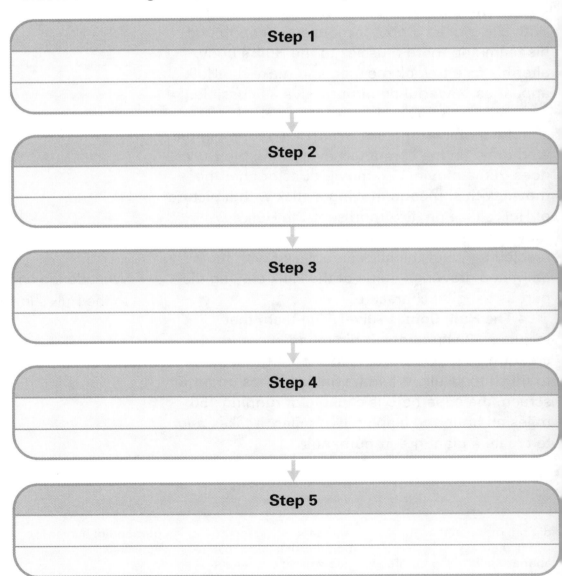

Step 1

Step 2

Step 3

Step 4

Step 5

Explore

It took lots of different people working together to create the animated Hulk, including artists, sculptors, technicians, and animators.

> **Fill in the concept map below to show how each group of people contributed to the project. In your descriptions, focus on how each group's task depended on the work done by the group before it. Use the information from the reading and in the chart on the previous page to help you.**

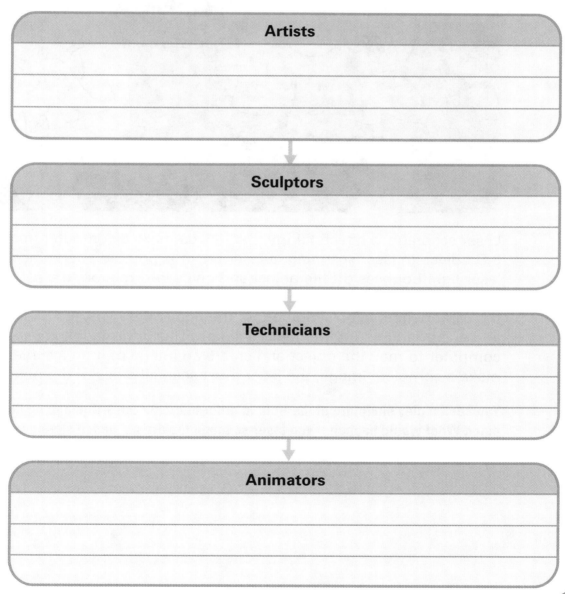

Artists

Sculptors

Technicians

Animators

Explore

MAKING A 3-D IMAGE

A pencil sketch shows an object in two dimensions (2-D). A clay sculpture shows an object in three dimensions (3-D). You can turn a sculpture around and see all sides of it. You can't see all sides of an object in a sketch.

Laser scanning is a technology that lets us make a computer image of a 3-D object. In laser scanning, a laser beam is pointed at an object. The laser light bounces off the object and gives information to a camera about how far away every part of the object is. A computer attached to the camera gets information about the ups and downs, ins and outs, and everything about the object's shape. This information is used by the computer to map the object and create an image of it on a screen. To make a complete image, the laser must scan all sides of the object.

> **You need a clay sculpture of the Hulk in order to create the 3-D image on the computer. What would happen if you laser-scanned the artists' pencil sketches instead?**

UNIT 5: Science, Technology, and Society

What Did We Learn?

What did wasps know about making paper long before people did?

How can technology improve the life of a wild animal that is injured?

What kinds of people are needed to create an animated movie character?

Glossary of Science Terms

A

adaptation: a structure or behavior that helps an organism meet its basic needs (36)

amphibian: an animal that lives in water when it is young and on land when it is an adult (135)

artificial: made by people (154)

astronomy: the study of planet Earth and objects in space

B

binoculars: a tool for observing objects that are far away

biodiversity: the variety of different species in an area (144)

brain: the organ in the nervous system that is the control center of the body

C

canyon: steep-sided river valley (65)

carnivore: an organism that eats animals (26)

cavern: a large cave

chemical change: a change that produces a new substance when two or more chemicals are combined to produce new chemicals (98)

chemical compound: a substance made up of two or more elements (89)

chemical property: the ability of a substance to react with other substances and to change into a new substance with different properties (93)

chemistry: the science of elements and chemical compounds (90)

classification system: a system that groups organisms based on similarities and differences of their traits (16)

computer: an electronic machine that stores and processes information

D

deformity: a body part that is not "normal" (133, 134)

dental technician: someone who makes devices for dentists (155)

deposition: the process in which rock eroded by water, wind, or ice is dropped in a new place (62)

digest: break food down into nutrients that the body can use

digital: made on the computer **(161)**

dinosaur: an extinct reptile that lived long ago

dissolve: to form a solution with another substance

dung: poop **(128)**

E

earthquake: movements of Earth's crust that produce waves that pass through Earth **(51)**

earth science: the study of planet Earth and objects in space

eclipse: one object in space casting its shadow on another object in space **(81)**

ecosystem: all the living and nonliving things that are found in an area **(43)**

electrical energy: a form of energy that is produced when negative electric charges move from one place to another place; also called *electricity* **(105)**

electricity: a form of energy that is produced when negative electric charges move from one place to another place; also called *electrical energy* **(101)**

element: the most basic kind of matter; a pure substance made of only one kind of atom **(89)**

embryo: the body of an unhatched animal **(72)**

energy: the ability to cause motion or change **(107)**

energy of motion: the energy of a moving object due to its motion; also called *kinetic energy* **(105, 111)**

engineer: someone who designs technology to solve problems **(150)**

environment: the surroundings that an organism lives in

erosion: the movement of weathered rock by water, wind, or ice **(62, 66)**

eruption: a sudden, violent outburst of lava or ash from a volcano

evaporate: to change from a liquid to a gas **(115, 116)**

evidence: proof; facts that support an idea

experiment: a scientific investigation that tests a hypothesis

extinction: the dying out of a species **(134)**

F

fertilizer: chemical used to help grass grow **(135)**

force: a push or pull

fossil: the remains or traces of an organism that lived long ago

friction: a force that makes it hard for two surfaces to slide past one another; friction works against motion **(112)**

fuel: a material that is burned to produce heat energy

G

generator: a device that uses magnets to change the energy of motion to electrical energy **(105)**

gravity: the force that pulls objects toward each other

H

heat energy: the energy of moving particles in a substance; also called *thermal energy*

herbal supplement: a product made from a type of leafy plant called an herb **(141)**

I

image: what you see at the place where an object would be if light rays reflecting off the object did not change direction slightly **(124)**

indicator species: a kind of plant or animal that reacts quickly to changes in the environment **(136)**

inference: an idea that explains an observation or answers a question **(71)**

inherit: receive characteristics that are passed from parents to their offspring **(40)**

insect: a small animal, such as a ladybug, that usually has six legs, two wings, and a hard shell

introduced species: species of plants and animals that have been brought to a new area **(43)**

invention: a new device usually designed from scientific knowledge or study

L

landform: a natural structure or feature on Earth's surface **(63)**

laser: concentrated light beam **(160)**

life science: the study of plants, animals, and all other living things; also called *biology*

light: a form of energy that travels in waves and can move through empty space where there is no air

M

machine: a tool that makes work easier, usually by letting you use less force

malaria: a serious tropical disease that gives people a high fever, which is caused by a germ that is carried by mosquitoes **(142)**

mammal: an animal that has a backbone and hair or fur, breathes with lungs, gives birth to live young, and feeds milk to its young

mate: to make more organisms of the same kind

mesa: flat-topped land with cliffs at the edges **(64)**

mineral: a solid natural material that has a crystal form and its own set of properties

motor: a device that uses electricity to produce motion

mutation: a change in traits that happens when the traits are being passed from parent to offspring **(41)**

N

native species: species of plants and animals that have lived in an area for a very long time **(43)**

natural resources: materials in the environment that are useful to people

nerve cell: a cell in the nervous system that carries messages to and from the spinal cord and brain

nutrients: substances that an organism needs in order to survive and grow

N

native species: species of plants and animals that have lived in an area for a very long time (43)

natural resources: materials in the environment that are useful to people

nerve cell: a cell in the nervous system that carries messages to and from the spinal cord and brain

nutrients: substances that an organism needs in order to survive and grow

O

observation: something that you note using your senses (71)

offspring: young organisms that come from parent organisms (37)

organism: a living thing

P

perpetual motion machine: an imaginary machine that runs forever without any outside energy (108)

pesticide: a chemical used to kill insects and other small animals (134)

phase (of the moon): one stage in the regular changes in the way the moon looks from Earth (82)

photosynthesis: the process of using the energy in sunlight to make food from water and carbon dioxide

physical science: the study of matter, forces, motion, and energy

plant fibers: tough strands of material found in all plants (150)

plate: a huge piece of Earth's crust that moves very slowly (56)

polluted: harmed or damaged by waste material that is not part of the natural environment

predator: an animal that catches and eats another animal (47)

prey: an animal that is hunted, caught, and eaten by another animal for food (47, 91)

prosthesis: an artificial body part used to replace a natural part that is damaged or missing (153)

prototype: an early model of a design (154, 156)

Q

quinine: a drug used to treat patients with malaria

R

reagent: a chemical that causes another chemical to change **(96)**

recycle: turn in waste items so the materials they are made of can be used to make new items

reflect: bounce back **(121)**

reflection: the bouncing back of light rays from a surface

refract: change direction slightly (light rays) **(124)**

refraction: the bending of light rays as they move from one material into another material

relief map: a map that shows features of the land by showing the shadows that they cast **(67)**

reproduce: to make more organisms of the same kind

S

scientist: someone who studies the natural world

seismograph: a science tool that measures the strength of earthquakes **(54)**

society: a group of people who all live under the same set of rules

solution: a mixture with one substance spread out so evenly in another substance that you cannot tell the two substances apart; liquid mixture **(96)**

species: one kind of living thing; a group of organisms of the same kind that can mate and produce offspring like themselves **(17, 134)**

stalactite: cave formation that extends down from the ceiling of a cavern

stalagmite: cave formation that rises from the floor of a cavern

stored energy: energy that is stored in an object due to its position; also called *potential energy* **(111)**

synthetic: made by people in the laboratory **(142)**

T

technology: any tool or product that helps people in some way and that was created using scientific knowledge **(118, 150, 153)**

telescope: a tool for observing distant objects

temperature: the average speed of the particles in a substance

thermometer: a tool that measures temperature

three-dimensional: an object, such as a sculpture, that has height, width, and depth

tool: a device used to make a job easier **(33)**

tornado: a funnel-shaped storm cloud caused by rotating, high-speed winds **(75)**

toxin: poison **(90)**

trait: a characteristic or feature of an organism **(16)**

tundra: regions where it is very cold and there are almost no trees **(128)**

V

vortex: a swirling, twirling, moving shape in water or air **(78)**

W

wave: a repeating up-and-down or back-and-forth movement of matter

weathering: the breaking down, dissolving, and wearing away of rock **(62, 66)**

Sources

The readings in the Science Daybook come from the following sources.

14 From *James and the Giant Peach* by Roald Dahl, Copyright 1961 by Roald Dahl. Text copyright renewed 1989 by Roald Dahl. Alfred A. Knopf, an imprint of Random House Children's Books, a division of Random House, Inc.

20 Reprinted by permission of Carus Publishing Company from MUSE magazine, February 2003, Vol. 7, No. 2, © 2003 by Carus Publishing Company.

26 *A Moment of Science* radio series, WFIU-FM, Indiana University.

32 *Science News for Kids*, March 26, 2003. (www.sciencenewsforkids.org)

34 From *Pets and Wildlife* column, Gary Bogue, *Contra Costa Times*, April 16, 2003.

38 From *The Enormous Egg* by Oliver Butterworth. Copyright © 1956 by Oliver Butterworth; Copyright © renewed 1984 by Oliver Butterworth. By permission of Little, Brown and Company, (Inc.).

44, 46 Reprinted by permission of Carus Publishing Company from ASK magazine, July/Aug 2003, Vol. 2, No. 4, © 2003 by Catherine Ripley.

52 From *Dragonwings* by Laurence Yep. Copyright © 1975 by Laurence Yep. Used by permission of Harper Collins Publishers.

58 Copyright *Richmond Times-Dispatch*, August 14, 2003. Used with permission.

64 Excerpt from *Sing Down the Moon* by Scott O'Dell. Copyright © 1970 by Scott O'Dell, renewed 1998 by Elizabeth Hall. Reprinted by permission of Houghton Mifflin Company. All rights reserved.

70, 72 From *Tracking Dinosaurs in the Gobi* by Margery Facklam. Copyright © 1997 by Margery Facklam. Twenty-First Century Books, a division of Henry Holt and Company, Inc. Reprinted by permission of Margery Facklam. All rights reserved.

76 From *Nature's Fury: Eyewitness Reports of Natural Disasters* by Carole Garbuny Vogel. Copyright © 2000 Carole Garbuny Vogel. Reprinted by permission of Scholastic, Inc.

82, 84 *Talk of the Nation: Science Friday*, May 9, 2003, second hour. National Public Radio.

90 *Science News for Kids*, Sept 10, 2003. (www.sciencenewsforkids.org)

96 Reprinted by permission of Carus Publishing Company from ASK magazine, January/February 2003, Vol. 2, No.1, text © 2002 by Carus Publishing Company, illustrations © 2002 by Dean Stanton.

102 *Science News for Kids*, Aug 27, 2003. (www.sciencenewsforkids.org)

108 Reprinted by permission of Carus Publishing Company from MUSE magazine, May/June 2003, Vol. 7, No. 5, © 2003 by David Lindley.

114 *A Moment of Science* radio series, WFIU-FM, Indiana University.

120 Excerpt from *Island of the Blue Dolphins* by Scott O'Dell. Copyright © 1960, renewed 1988 by Scott O'Dell. Reprinted by permission of Houghton Mifflin Company. All rights reserved.

122 From *Call It Courage* by Armstrong Sperry. Copyright 1940 by Macmillan Publishing Company. Copyright renewed by Armstrong Sperry. Reprinted by permission of the Armstrong Sperry estate.

128 *Science News for Kids,* August 13, 2003. (www.sciencenewsforkids.org)

134 National Geographic Society, *National Geographic World,* March 2002.

140 "Silly Pilly" from *Laugh-Eteria,* copyright

© 1999 by Douglas Florian, reprinted by permission of Harcourt, Inc.

142 From *Accidents May Happen* by Charlotte Foltz Jones. Illustrations by John O'Brien, copyright © 1996 by Charlotte Foltz Jones. Used by permission of Random House Children's Books, a division of Random House, Inc.

148 From *Accidents May Happen* by Charlotte Foltz Jones. Illustrations by John O'Brien, copyright © 1996 by Charlotte Foltz Jones. Used by permission of Random House Children's Books, a division of Random House, Inc.

154 Reuters News Service. *Planet Ark,* August 19, 2002.

160 National Geographic Society, *National Geographic Kids,* July/August 2003.

The editors have made every effort to trace the ownership of all copyrighted selections found in this book and to make full acknowledgment for their use. Omissions brought to our attention will be corrected in a subsequent edition.